PERSONAL DETAIL

NAME

ADDRESS

EMAIL

PHONE NUMBER

NOTARY LOG BOOK DETAILS

LOG START DATE

LOG BOOK NUMBER

NOTARY LOG

FULL NAME:	PHONE NUMBER:	THUMB PRINT
EMAIL ADDRESS:	SIGNER'S SIGNATURE	
ADDRESS:		

SERVICE PERFORMED:	IDENTIFICATION	ID NUMBER:
❑ JURAT	❑ ID CARD ❑ CREDIBLE WITNESS ❑ KNOWN PERSONALLY	
❑ OATH	❑ PASSPORT	ISSUED BY:
❑ ACKNOWLEDGEMENT	❑ DRIVER'S LICENSE	
❑ OTHER: _____	❑ OTHER: _____	DATE ISSUED: / EXPIRATION DATE:

WITNESS FULL NAME:	PHONE NUMBER:
EMAIL ADDRESS:	WITNESS SIGNATURE:
ADDRESS:	

DOCUMENT TYPE:	DATE/TIME NOTARIZED:	DOCUMENT DATE:	FEE CHARGED:

COMMENTS:		RECORD NUMBER: 1

NOTARY LOG

FULL NAME:	PHONE NUMBER:	THUMB PRINT
EMAIL ADDRESS:	SIGNER'S SIGNATURE	
ADDRESS:		

SERVICE PERFORMED:	IDENTIFICATION	ID NUMBER:
❑ JURAT	❑ ID CARD ❑ CREDIBLE WITNESS ❑ KNOWN PERSONALLY	
❑ OATH	❑ PASSPORT	ISSUED BY:
❑ ACKNOWLEDGEMENT	❑ DRIVER'S LICENSE	
❑ OTHER: _____	❑ OTHER: _____	DATE ISSUED: / EXPIRATION DATE:

WITNESS FULL NAME:	PHONE NUMBER:
EMAIL ADDRESS:	WITNESS SIGNATURE:
ADDRESS:	

DOCUMENT TYPE:	DATE/TIME NOTARIZED:	DOCUMENT DATE:	FEE CHARGED:

COMMENTS:		RECORD NUMBER: 2

NOTARY LOG

FULL NAME:	PHONE NUMBER:	THUMB PRINT
EMAIL ADDRESS:	SIGNER'S SIGNATURE	
ADDRESS:		

SERVICE PERFORMED:
- ❑ JURAT
- ❑ OATH
- ❑ ACKNOWLEDGEMENT
- ❑ OTHER: _____

IDENTIFICATION
- ❑ ID CARD
- ❑ PASSPORT
- ❑ DRIVER'S LICENSE
- ❑ OTHER: _____
- ❑ CREDIBLE WITNESS
- ❑ KNOWN PERSONALLY

ID NUMBER:

ISSUED BY:

DATE ISSUED:	EXPIRATION DATE:

WITNESS FULL NAME:	PHONE NUMBER:
EMAIL ADDRESS:	WITNESS SIGNATURE:
ADDRESS:	

DOCUMENT TYPE:	DATE/TIME NOTARIZED:	DOCUMENT DATE:	FEE CHARGED:

COMMENTS:		RECORD NUMBER: 3

NOTARY LOG

FULL NAME:	PHONE NUMBER:	THUMB PRINT
EMAIL ADDRESS:	SIGNER'S SIGNATURE	
ADDRESS:		

SERVICE PERFORMED:
- ❑ JURAT
- ❑ OATH
- ❑ ACKNOWLEDGEMENT
- ❑ OTHER: _____

IDENTIFICATION
- ❑ ID CARD
- ❑ PASSPORT
- ❑ DRIVER'S LICENSE
- ❑ OTHER: _____
- ❑ CREDIBLE WITNESS
- ❑ KNOWN PERSONALLY

ID NUMBER:

ISSUED BY:

DATE ISSUED:	EXPIRATION DATE:

WITNESS FULL NAME:	PHONE NUMBER:
EMAIL ADDRESS:	WITNESS SIGNATURE:
ADDRESS:	

DOCUMENT TYPE:	DATE/TIME NOTARIZED:	DOCUMENT DATE:	FEE CHARGED:

COMMENTS:		RECORD NUMBER: 4

NOTARY LOG

FULL NAME:	PHONE NUMBER:	THUMB PRINT
EMAIL ADDRESS:	SIGNER'S SIGNATURE	
ADDRESS:		

SERVICE PERFORMED:	IDENTIFICATION		ID NUMBER:
☐ JURAT	☐ ID CARD	☐ CREDIBLE WITNESS	
☐ OATH	☐ PASSPORT	☐ KNOWN PERSONALLY	ISSUED BY:
☐ ACKNOWLEDGEMENT	☐ DRIVER'S LICENSE		
☐ OTHER: _____	☐ OTHER: _____	DATE ISSUED:	EXPIRATION DATE:

WITNESS FULL NAME:	PHONE NUMBER:
EMAIL ADDRESS:	WITNESS SIGNATURE:
ADDRESS:	

DOCUMENT TYPE:	DATE/TIME NOTARIZED:	DOCUMENT DATE:	FEE CHARGED:
COMMENTS:		RECORD NUMBER:	5

NOTARY LOG

FULL NAME:	PHONE NUMBER:	THUMB PRINT
EMAIL ADDRESS:	SIGNER'S SIGNATURE	
ADDRESS:		

SERVICE PERFORMED:	IDENTIFICATION		ID NUMBER:
☐ JURAT	☐ ID CARD	☐ CREDIBLE WITNESS	
☐ OATH	☐ PASSPORT	☐ KNOWN PERSONALLY	ISSUED BY:
☐ ACKNOWLEDGEMENT	☐ DRIVER'S LICENSE		
☐ OTHER: _____	☐ OTHER: _____	DATE ISSUED:	EXPIRATION DATE:

WITNESS FULL NAME:	PHONE NUMBER:
EMAIL ADDRESS:	WITNESS SIGNATURE:
ADDRESS:	

DOCUMENT TYPE:	DATE/TIME NOTARIZED:	DOCUMENT DATE:	FEE CHARGED:
COMMENTS:		RECORD NUMBER:	6

NOTARY LOG

FULL NAME:	PHONE NUMBER:	THUMB PRINT
EMAIL ADDRESS:	SIGNER'S SIGNATURE	
ADDRESS:		

SERVICE PERFORMED:	IDENTIFICATION	ID NUMBER:
❑ JURAT	❑ ID CARD ❑ CREDIBLE WITNESS	
❑ OATH	❑ PASSPORT ❑ KNOWN PERSONALLY	ISSUED BY:
❑ ACKNOWLEDGEMENT	❑ DRIVER'S LICENSE	
❑ OTHER: _____	❑ OTHER: _____	DATE ISSUED: EXPIRATION DATE:

WITNESS FULL NAME:	PHONE NUMBER:
EMAIL ADDRESS:	WITNESS SIGNATURE:
ADDRESS:	

DOCUMENT TYPE:	DATE/TIME NOTARIZED:	DOCUMENT DATE:	FEE CHARGED:
COMMENTS:			RECORD NUMBER: 7

NOTARY LOG

FULL NAME:	PHONE NUMBER:	THUMB PRINT
EMAIL ADDRESS:	SIGNER'S SIGNATURE	
ADDRESS:		

SERVICE PERFORMED:	IDENTIFICATION	ID NUMBER:
❑ JURAT	❑ ID CARD ❑ CREDIBLE WITNESS	
❑ OATH	❑ PASSPORT ❑ KNOWN PERSONALLY	ISSUED BY:
❑ ACKNOWLEDGEMENT	❑ DRIVER'S LICENSE	
❑ OTHER: _____	❑ OTHER: _____	DATE ISSUED: EXPIRATION DATE:

WITNESS FULL NAME:	PHONE NUMBER:
EMAIL ADDRESS:	WITNESS SIGNATURE:
ADDRESS:	

DOCUMENT TYPE:	DATE/TIME NOTARIZED:	DOCUMENT DATE:	FEE CHARGED:
COMMENTS:			RECORD NUMBER: 8

NOTARY LOG

FULL NAME:	PHONE NUMBER:	THUMB PRINT
EMAIL ADDRESS:	SIGNER'S SIGNATURE	
ADDRESS:		

SERVICE PERFORMED:	IDENTIFICATION	ID NUMBER:
❑ JURAT	❑ ID CARD ❑ CREDIBLE WITNESS	
❑ OATH	❑ PASSPORT ❑ KNOWN PERSONALLY	ISSUED BY:
❑ ACKNOWLEDGEMENT	❑ DRIVER'S LICENSE	
❑ OTHER: _____	❑ OTHER: _____	DATE ISSUED: EXPIRATION DATE:

WITNESS FULL NAME:	PHONE NUMBER:
EMAIL ADDRESS:	WITNESS SIGNATURE:
ADDRESS:	

DOCUMENT TYPE:	DATE/TIME NOTARIZED:	DOCUMENT DATE:	FEE CHARGED:
COMMENTS:			RECORD NUMBER: **9**

NOTARY LOG

FULL NAME:	PHONE NUMBER:	THUMB PRINT
EMAIL ADDRESS:	SIGNER'S SIGNATURE	
ADDRESS:		

SERVICE PERFORMED:	IDENTIFICATION	ID NUMBER:
❑ JURAT	❑ ID CARD ❑ CREDIBLE WITNESS	
❑ OATH	❑ PASSPORT ❑ KNOWN PERSONALLY	ISSUED BY:
❑ ACKNOWLEDGEMENT	❑ DRIVER'S LICENSE	
❑ OTHER: _____	❑ OTHER: _____	DATE ISSUED: EXPIRATION DATE:

WITNESS FULL NAME:	PHONE NUMBER:
EMAIL ADDRESS:	WITNESS SIGNATURE:
ADDRESS:	

DOCUMENT TYPE:	DATE/TIME NOTARIZED:	DOCUMENT DATE:	FEE CHARGED:
COMMENTS:			RECORD NUMBER: **10**

NOTARY LOG

FULL NAME:	PHONE NUMBER:	THUMB PRINT
EMAIL ADDRESS:	SIGNER'S SIGNATURE	
ADDRESS:		

SERVICE PERFORMED:	IDENTIFICATION	ID NUMBER:
❑ JURAT	❑ ID CARD ❑ CREDIBLE WITNESS	
❑ OATH	❑ PASSPORT ❑ KNOWN PERSONALLY	ISSUED BY:
❑ ACKNOWLEDGEMENT	❑ DRIVER'S LICENSE	
❑ OTHER: _____	❑ OTHER: _____	DATE ISSUED: / EXPIRATION DATE:

WITNESS FULL NAME:	PHONE NUMBER:
EMAIL ADDRESS:	WITNESS SIGNATURE:
ADDRESS:	

DOCUMENT TYPE:	DATE/TIME NOTARIZED:	DOCUMENT DATE:	FEE CHARGED:
COMMENTS:			RECORD NUMBER: **11**

NOTARY LOG

FULL NAME:	PHONE NUMBER:	THUMB PRINT
EMAIL ADDRESS:	SIGNER'S SIGNATURE	
ADDRESS:		

SERVICE PERFORMED:	IDENTIFICATION	ID NUMBER:
❑ JURAT	❑ ID CARD ❑ CREDIBLE WITNESS	
❑ OATH	❑ PASSPORT ❑ KNOWN PERSONALLY	ISSUED BY:
❑ ACKNOWLEDGEMENT	❑ DRIVER'S LICENSE	
❑ OTHER: _____	❑ OTHER: _____	DATE ISSUED: / EXPIRATION DATE:

WITNESS FULL NAME:	PHONE NUMBER:
EMAIL ADDRESS:	WITNESS SIGNATURE:
ADDRESS:	

DOCUMENT TYPE:	DATE/TIME NOTARIZED:	DOCUMENT DATE:	FEE CHARGED:
COMMENTS:			RECORD NUMBER: **12**

NOTARY LOG

FULL NAME:		PHONE NUMBER:	THUMB PRINT
EMAIL ADDRESS:		SIGNER'S SIGNATURE	
ADDRESS:			

SERVICE PERFORMED:
- ☐ JURAT
- ☐ OATH
- ☐ ACKNOWLEDGEMENT
- ☐ OTHER: _____

IDENTIFICATION
- ☐ ID CARD
- ☐ PASSPORT
- ☐ DRIVER'S LICENSE
- ☐ OTHER: _____
- ☐ CREDIBLE WITNESS
- ☐ KNOWN PERSONALLY

ID NUMBER:

ISSUED BY:

DATE ISSUED: | EXPIRATION DATE:

WITNESS FULL NAME:	PHONE NUMBER:
EMAIL ADDRESS:	WITNESS SIGNATURE:
ADDRESS:	

DOCUMENT TYPE:	DATE/TIME NOTARIZED:	DOCUMENT DATE:	FEE CHARGED:
COMMENTS:			RECORD NUMBER: **13**

NOTARY LOG

FULL NAME:		PHONE NUMBER:	THUMB PRINT
EMAIL ADDRESS:		SIGNER'S SIGNATURE	
ADDRESS:			

SERVICE PERFORMED:
- ☐ JURAT
- ☐ OATH
- ☐ ACKNOWLEDGEMENT
- ☐ OTHER: _____

IDENTIFICATION
- ☐ ID CARD
- ☐ PASSPORT
- ☐ DRIVER'S LICENSE
- ☐ OTHER: _____
- ☐ CREDIBLE WITNESS
- ☐ KNOWN PERSONALLY

ID NUMBER:

ISSUED BY:

DATE ISSUED: | EXPIRATION DATE:

WITNESS FULL NAME:	PHONE NUMBER:
EMAIL ADDRESS:	WITNESS SIGNATURE:
ADDRESS:	

DOCUMENT TYPE:	DATE/TIME NOTARIZED:	DOCUMENT DATE:	FEE CHARGED:
COMMENTS:			RECORD NUMBER: **14**

NOTARY LOG

FULL NAME:	PHONE NUMBER:	THUMB PRINT
EMAIL ADDRESS:	SIGNER'S SIGNATURE	
ADDRESS:		

SERVICE PERFORMED:	IDENTIFICATION		ID NUMBER:
❑ JURAT	❑ ID CARD	❑ CREDIBLE WITNESS	
❑ OATH	❑ PASSPORT	❑ KNOWN PERSONALLY	ISSUED BY:
❑ ACKNOWLEDGEMENT	❑ DRIVER'S LICENSE		
❑ OTHER: _____	❑ OTHER: _____		DATE ISSUED: / EXPIRATION DATE:

WITNESS FULL NAME:	PHONE NUMBER:
EMAIL ADDRESS:	WITNESS SIGNATURE:
ADDRESS:	

DOCUMENT TYPE:	DATE/TIME NOTARIZED:	DOCUMENT DATE:	FEE CHARGED:
COMMENTS:			RECORD NUMBER: **15**

NOTARY LOG

FULL NAME:	PHONE NUMBER:	THUMB PRINT
EMAIL ADDRESS:	SIGNER'S SIGNATURE	
ADDRESS:		

SERVICE PERFORMED:	IDENTIFICATION		ID NUMBER:
❑ JURAT	❑ ID CARD	❑ CREDIBLE WITNESS	
❑ OATH	❑ PASSPORT	❑ KNOWN PERSONALLY	ISSUED BY:
❑ ACKNOWLEDGEMENT	❑ DRIVER'S LICENSE		
❑ OTHER: _____	❑ OTHER: _____		DATE ISSUED: / EXPIRATION DATE:

WITNESS FULL NAME:	PHONE NUMBER:
EMAIL ADDRESS:	WITNESS SIGNATURE:
ADDRESS:	

DOCUMENT TYPE:	DATE/TIME NOTARIZED:	DOCUMENT DATE:	FEE CHARGED:
COMMENTS:			RECORD NUMBER: **16**

NOTARY LOG

FULL NAME:	PHONE NUMBER:	THUMB PRINT
EMAIL ADDRESS:	SIGNER'S SIGNATURE	
ADDRESS:		

SERVICE PERFORMED:
- ❑ JURAT
- ❑ OATH
- ❑ ACKNOWLEDGEMENT
- ❑ OTHER: _____

IDENTIFICATION
- ❑ ID CARD
- ❑ PASSPORT
- ❑ DRIVER'S LICENSE
- ❑ OTHER: _____
- ❑ CREDIBLE WITNESS
- ❑ KNOWN PERSONALLY

ID NUMBER:

ISSUED BY:

DATE ISSUED: | EXPIRATION DATE:

WITNESS FULL NAME:	PHONE NUMBER:
EMAIL ADDRESS:	WITNESS SIGNATURE:
ADDRESS:	

DOCUMENT TYPE:	DATE/TIME NOTARIZED:	DOCUMENT DATE:	FEE CHARGED:

COMMENTS: | RECORD NUMBER: **17**

NOTARY LOG

FULL NAME:	PHONE NUMBER:	THUMB PRINT
EMAIL ADDRESS:	SIGNER'S SIGNATURE	
ADDRESS:		

SERVICE PERFORMED:
- ❑ JURAT
- ❑ OATH
- ❑ ACKNOWLEDGEMENT
- ❑ OTHER: _____

IDENTIFICATION
- ❑ ID CARD
- ❑ PASSPORT
- ❑ DRIVER'S LICENSE
- ❑ OTHER: _____
- ❑ CREDIBLE WITNESS
- ❑ KNOWN PERSONALLY

ID NUMBER:

ISSUED BY:

DATE ISSUED: | EXPIRATION DATE:

WITNESS FULL NAME:	PHONE NUMBER:
EMAIL ADDRESS:	WITNESS SIGNATURE:
ADDRESS:	

DOCUMENT TYPE:	DATE/TIME NOTARIZED:	DOCUMENT DATE:	FEE CHARGED:

COMMENTS: | RECORD NUMBER: **18**

NOTARY LOG

FULL NAME:	PHONE NUMBER:	THUMB PRINT
EMAIL ADDRESS:	SIGNER'S SIGNATURE	
ADDRESS:		

SERVICE PERFORMED:	IDENTIFICATION	ID NUMBER:
❏ JURAT	❏ ID CARD ❏ CREDIBLE WITNESS	
❏ OATH	❏ PASSPORT ❏ KNOWN PERSONALLY	ISSUED BY:
❏ ACKNOWLEDGEMENT	❏ DRIVER'S LICENSE	
❏ OTHER: _____	❏ OTHER: _____	DATE ISSUED: / EXPIRATION DATE:

WITNESS FULL NAME:	PHONE NUMBER:
EMAIL ADDRESS:	WITNESS SIGNATURE:
ADDRESS:	

DOCUMENT TYPE:	DATE/TIME NOTARIZED:	DOCUMENT DATE:	FEE CHARGED:

COMMENTS:		RECORD NUMBER: 19

NOTARY LOG

FULL NAME:	PHONE NUMBER:	THUMB PRINT
EMAIL ADDRESS:	SIGNER'S SIGNATURE	
ADDRESS:		

SERVICE PERFORMED:	IDENTIFICATION	ID NUMBER:
❏ JURAT	❏ ID CARD ❏ CREDIBLE WITNESS	
❏ OATH	❏ PASSPORT ❏ KNOWN PERSONALLY	ISSUED BY:
❏ ACKNOWLEDGEMENT	❏ DRIVER'S LICENSE	
❏ OTHER: _____	❏ OTHER: _____	DATE ISSUED: EXPIRATION DATE:

WITNESS FULL NAME:	PHONE NUMBER:
EMAIL ADDRESS:	WITNESS SIGNATURE:
ADDRESS:	

DOCUMENT TYPE:	DATE/TIME NOTARIZED:	DOCUMENT DATE:	FEE CHARGED:

COMMENTS:		RECORD NUMBER: 20

NOTARY LOG

FULL NAME:	PHONE NUMBER:	THUMB PRINT
EMAIL ADDRESS:	SIGNER'S SIGNATURE	
ADDRESS:		

SERVICE PERFORMED:	IDENTIFICATION		ID NUMBER:
❑ JURAT	❑ ID CARD	❑ CREDIBLE WITNESS	
❑ OATH	❑ PASSPORT	❑ KNOWN PERSONALLY	ISSUED BY:
❑ ACKNOWLEDGEMENT	❑ DRIVER'S LICENSE		
❑ OTHER: _____	❑ OTHER: _____		DATE ISSUED: / EXPIRATION DATE:

WITNESS FULL NAME:	PHONE NUMBER:
EMAIL ADDRESS:	WITNESS SIGNATURE:
ADDRESS:	

DOCUMENT TYPE:	DATE/TIME NOTARIZED:	DOCUMENT DATE:	FEE CHARGED:
COMMENTS:			RECORD NUMBER: **21**

NOTARY LOG

FULL NAME:	PHONE NUMBER:	THUMB PRINT
EMAIL ADDRESS:	SIGNER'S SIGNATURE	
ADDRESS:		

SERVICE PERFORMED:	IDENTIFICATION		ID NUMBER:
❑ JURAT	❑ ID CARD	❑ CREDIBLE WITNESS	
❑ OATH	❑ PASSPORT	❑ KNOWN PERSONALLY	ISSUED BY:
❑ ACKNOWLEDGEMENT	❑ DRIVER'S LICENSE		
❑ OTHER: _____	❑ OTHER: _____		DATE ISSUED: / EXPIRATION DATE:

WITNESS FULL NAME:	PHONE NUMBER:
EMAIL ADDRESS:	WITNESS SIGNATURE:
ADDRESS:	

DOCUMENT TYPE:	DATE/TIME NOTARIZED:	DOCUMENT DATE:	FEE CHARGED:
COMMENTS:			RECORD NUMBER: **22**

NOTARY LOG

FULL NAME:	PHONE NUMBER:	THUMB PRINT
EMAIL ADDRESS:	SIGNER'S SIGNATURE	
ADDRESS:		

SERVICE PERFORMED:
- ❏ JURAT
- ❏ OATH
- ❏ ACKNOWLEDGEMENT
- ❏ OTHER: _____

IDENTIFICATION
- ❏ ID CARD
- ❏ PASSPORT
- ❏ DRIVER'S LICENSE
- ❏ OTHER: _____
- ❏ CREDIBLE WITNESS
- ❏ KNOWN PERSONALLY

ID NUMBER:

ISSUED BY:

DATE ISSUED:	EXPIRATION DATE:

WITNESS FULL NAME:	PHONE NUMBER:
EMAIL ADDRESS:	WITNESS SIGNATURE:
ADDRESS:	

DOCUMENT TYPE:	DATE/TIME NOTARIZED:	DOCUMENT DATE:	FEE CHARGED:

COMMENTS:		RECORD NUMBER: **23**

NOTARY LOG

FULL NAME:	PHONE NUMBER:	THUMB PRINT
EMAIL ADDRESS:	SIGNER'S SIGNATURE	
ADDRESS:		

SERVICE PERFORMED:
- ❏ JURAT
- ❏ OATH
- ❏ ACKNOWLEDGEMENT
- ❏ OTHER: _____

IDENTIFICATION
- ❏ ID CARD
- ❏ PASSPORT
- ❏ DRIVER'S LICENSE
- ❏ OTHER: _____
- ❏ CREDIBLE WITNESS
- ❏ KNOWN PERSONALLY

ID NUMBER:

ISSUED BY:

DATE ISSUED:	EXPIRATION DATE:

WITNESS FULL NAME:	PHONE NUMBER:
EMAIL ADDRESS:	WITNESS SIGNATURE:
ADDRESS:	

DOCUMENT TYPE:	DATE/TIME NOTARIZED:	DOCUMENT DATE:	FEE CHARGED:

COMMENTS:		RECORD NUMBER: **24**

NOTARY LOG

FULL NAME:

PHONE NUMBER:

THUMB PRINT

EMAIL ADDRESS:

SIGNER'S SIGNATURE

ADDRESS:

SERVICE PERFORMED:

- ❏ JURAT
- ❏ OATH
- ❏ ACKNOWLEDGEMENT
- ❏ OTHER: _____

IDENTIFICATION

- ❏ ID CARD
- ❏ PASSPORT
- ❏ DRIVER'S LICENSE
- ❏ OTHER: _____
- ❏ CREDIBLE WITNESS
- ❏ KNOWN PERSONALLY

ID NUMBER:

ISSUED BY:

DATE ISSUED:

EXPIRATION DATE:

WITNESS FULL NAME:

PHONE NUMBER:

EMAIL ADDRESS:

WITNESS SIGNATURE:

ADDRESS:

DOCUMENT TYPE:	DATE/TIME NOTARIZED:	DOCUMENT DATE:	FEE CHARGED:

COMMENTS:

RECORD NUMBER: 25

NOTARY LOG

FULL NAME:

PHONE NUMBER:

THUMB PRINT

EMAIL ADDRESS:

SIGNER'S SIGNATURE

ADDRESS:

SERVICE PERFORMED:

- ❏ JURAT
- ❏ OATH
- ❏ ACKNOWLEDGEMENT
- ❏ OTHER: _____

IDENTIFICATION

- ❏ ID CARD
- ❏ PASSPORT
- ❏ DRIVER'S LICENSE
- ❏ OTHER: _____
- ❏ CREDIBLE WITNESS
- ❏ KNOWN PERSONALLY

ID NUMBER:

ISSUED BY:

DATE ISSUED:

EXPIRATION DATE:

WITNESS FULL NAME:

PHONE NUMBER:

EMAIL ADDRESS:

WITNESS SIGNATURE:

ADDRESS:

DOCUMENT TYPE:	DATE/TIME NOTARIZED:	DOCUMENT DATE:	FEE CHARGED:

COMMENTS:

RECORD NUMBER: 26

NOTARY LOG

FULL NAME:	PHONE NUMBER:	THUMB PRINT

EMAIL ADDRESS:	SIGNER'S SIGNATURE
ADDRESS:	

SERVICE PERFORMED:
- ❑ JURAT
- ❑ OATH
- ❑ ACKNOWLEDGEMENT
- ❑ OTHER: _____

IDENTIFICATION
- ❑ ID CARD
- ❑ PASSPORT
- ❑ DRIVER'S LICENSE
- ❑ OTHER: _____
- ❑ CREDIBLE WITNESS
- ❑ KNOWN PERSONALLY

ID NUMBER:

ISSUED BY:

DATE ISSUED:	EXPIRATION DATE:

WITNESS FULL NAME:	PHONE NUMBER:

EMAIL ADDRESS:	WITNESS SIGNATURE:
ADDRESS:	

DOCUMENT TYPE:	DATE/TIME NOTARIZED:	DOCUMENT DATE:	FEE CHARGED:

COMMENTS:		RECORD NUMBER: **27**

NOTARY LOG

FULL NAME:	PHONE NUMBER:	THUMB PRINT

EMAIL ADDRESS:	SIGNER'S SIGNATURE
ADDRESS:	

SERVICE PERFORMED:
- ❑ JURAT
- ❑ OATH
- ❑ ACKNOWLEDGEMENT
- ❑ OTHER: _____

IDENTIFICATION
- ❑ ID CARD
- ❑ PASSPORT
- ❑ DRIVER'S LICENSE
- ❑ OTHER: _____
- ❑ CREDIBLE WITNESS
- ❑ KNOWN PERSONALLY

ID NUMBER:

ISSUED BY:

DATE ISSUED:	EXPIRATION DATE:

WITNESS FULL NAME:	PHONE NUMBER:

EMAIL ADDRESS:	WITNESS SIGNATURE:
ADDRESS:	

DOCUMENT TYPE:	DATE/TIME NOTARIZED:	DOCUMENT DATE:	FEE CHARGED:

COMMENTS:		RECORD NUMBER: **28**

NOTARY LOG

FULL NAME:	PHONE NUMBER:	THUMB PRINT
EMAIL ADDRESS:	SIGNER'S SIGNATURE	
ADDRESS:		

SERVICE PERFORMED:	IDENTIFICATION	ID NUMBER:
❑ JURAT	❑ ID CARD ❑ CREDIBLE WITNESS	
❑ OATH	❑ PASSPORT ❑ KNOWN PERSONALLY	ISSUED BY:
❑ ACKNOWLEDGEMENT	❑ DRIVER'S LICENSE	
❑ OTHER: _____	❑ OTHER: _____	DATE ISSUED: EXPIRATION DATE:

WITNESS FULL NAME:	PHONE NUMBER:
EMAIL ADDRESS:	WITNESS SIGNATURE:
ADDRESS:	

DOCUMENT TYPE:	DATE/TIME NOTARIZED:	DOCUMENT DATE:	FEE CHARGED:

COMMENTS:		RECORD NUMBER: **29**

NOTARY LOG

FULL NAME:	PHONE NUMBER:	THUMB PRINT
EMAIL ADDRESS:	SIGNER'S SIGNATURE	
ADDRESS:		

SERVICE PERFORMED:	IDENTIFICATION	ID NUMBER:
❑ JURAT	❑ ID CARD ❑ CREDIBLE WITNESS	
❑ OATH	❑ PASSPORT ❑ KNOWN PERSONALLY	ISSUED BY:
❑ ACKNOWLEDGEMENT	❑ DRIVER'S LICENSE	
❑ OTHER: _____	❑ OTHER: _____	DATE ISSUED: EXPIRATION DATE:

WITNESS FULL NAME:	PHONE NUMBER:
EMAIL ADDRESS:	WITNESS SIGNATURE:
ADDRESS:	

DOCUMENT TYPE:	DATE/TIME NOTARIZED:	DOCUMENT DATE:	FEE CHARGED:

COMMENTS:		RECORD NUMBER: **30**

NOTARY LOG

FULL NAME:	PHONE NUMBER:	THUMB PRINT
EMAIL ADDRESS:	SIGNER'S SIGNATURE	
ADDRESS:		

SERVICE PERFORMED:	IDENTIFICATION	ID NUMBER:
❑ JURAT	❑ ID CARD ❑ CREDIBLE WITNESS	
❑ OATH	❑ PASSPORT ❑ KNOWN PERSONALLY	ISSUED BY:
❑ ACKNOWLEDGEMENT	❑ DRIVER'S LICENSE	
❑ OTHER: _____	❑ OTHER: _____	DATE ISSUED: / EXPIRATION DATE:

WITNESS FULL NAME:	PHONE NUMBER:
EMAIL ADDRESS:	WITNESS SIGNATURE:
ADDRESS:	

DOCUMENT TYPE:	DATE/TIME NOTARIZED:	DOCUMENT DATE:	FEE CHARGED:
COMMENTS:			RECORD NUMBER: 31

NOTARY LOG

FULL NAME:	PHONE NUMBER:	THUMB PRINT
EMAIL ADDRESS:	SIGNER'S SIGNATURE	
ADDRESS:		

SERVICE PERFORMED:	IDENTIFICATION	ID NUMBER:
❑ JURAT	❑ ID CARD ❑ CREDIBLE WITNESS	
❑ OATH	❑ PASSPORT ❑ KNOWN PERSONALLY	ISSUED BY:
❑ ACKNOWLEDGEMENT	❑ DRIVER'S LICENSE	
❑ OTHER: _____	❑ OTHER: _____	DATE ISSUED: / EXPIRATION DATE:

WITNESS FULL NAME:	PHONE NUMBER:
EMAIL ADDRESS:	WITNESS SIGNATURE:
ADDRESS:	

DOCUMENT TYPE:	DATE/TIME NOTARIZED:	DOCUMENT DATE:	FEE CHARGED:
COMMENTS:			RECORD NUMBER: 32

NOTARY LOG

FULL NAME:	PHONE NUMBER:	THUMB PRINT
EMAIL ADDRESS:	SIGNER'S SIGNATURE	
ADDRESS:		

SERVICE PERFORMED:
- ❑ JURAT
- ❑ OATH
- ❑ ACKNOWLEDGEMENT
- ❑ OTHER: _____

IDENTIFICATION
- ❑ ID CARD
- ❑ PASSPORT
- ❑ DRIVER'S LICENSE
- ❑ OTHER: _____
- ❑ CREDIBLE WITNESS
- ❑ KNOWN PERSONALLY

ID NUMBER:

ISSUED BY:

DATE ISSUED: | EXPIRATION DATE:

WITNESS FULL NAME:	PHONE NUMBER:
EMAIL ADDRESS:	WITNESS SIGNATURE:
ADDRESS:	

DOCUMENT TYPE:	DATE/TIME NOTARIZED:	DOCUMENT DATE:	FEE CHARGED:

COMMENTS:		RECORD NUMBER: **33**

NOTARY LOG

FULL NAME:	PHONE NUMBER:	THUMB PRINT
EMAIL ADDRESS:	SIGNER'S SIGNATURE	
ADDRESS:		

SERVICE PERFORMED:
- ❑ JURAT
- ❑ OATH
- ❑ ACKNOWLEDGEMENT
- ❑ OTHER: _____

IDENTIFICATION
- ❑ ID CARD
- ❑ PASSPORT
- ❑ DRIVER'S LICENSE
- ❑ OTHER: _____
- ❑ CREDIBLE WITNESS
- ❑ KNOWN PERSONALLY

ID NUMBER:

ISSUED BY:

DATE ISSUED: | EXPIRATION DATE:

WITNESS FULL NAME:	PHONE NUMBER:
EMAIL ADDRESS:	WITNESS SIGNATURE:
ADDRESS:	

DOCUMENT TYPE:	DATE/TIME NOTARIZED:	DOCUMENT DATE:	FEE CHARGED:

COMMENTS:		RECORD NUMBER: **34**

NOTARY LOG

FULL NAME:	PHONE NUMBER:	THUMB PRINT
EMAIL ADDRESS:	SIGNER'S SIGNATURE	
ADDRESS:		

SERVICE PERFORMED:	IDENTIFICATION		ID NUMBER:
❑ JURAT	❑ ID CARD	❑ CREDIBLE WITNESS	
❑ OATH	❑ PASSPORT	❑ KNOWN PERSONALLY	ISSUED BY:
❑ ACKNOWLEDGEMENT	❑ DRIVER'S LICENSE		
❑ OTHER: _____	❑ OTHER: _____		DATE ISSUED: / EXPIRATION DATE:

WITNESS FULL NAME:	PHONE NUMBER:
EMAIL ADDRESS:	WITNESS SIGNATURE:
ADDRESS:	

DOCUMENT TYPE:	DATE/TIME NOTARIZED:	DOCUMENT DATE:	FEE CHARGED:
COMMENTS:			RECORD NUMBER: 35

NOTARY LOG

FULL NAME:	PHONE NUMBER:	THUMB PRINT
EMAIL ADDRESS:	SIGNER'S SIGNATURE	
ADDRESS:		

SERVICE PERFORMED:	IDENTIFICATION		ID NUMBER:
❑ JURAT	❑ ID CARD	❑ CREDIBLE WITNESS	
❑ OATH	❑ PASSPORT	❑ KNOWN PERSONALLY	ISSUED BY:
❑ ACKNOWLEDGEMENT	❑ DRIVER'S LICENSE		
❑ OTHER: _____	❑ OTHER: _____		DATE ISSUED: / EXPIRATION DATE:

WITNESS FULL NAME:	PHONE NUMBER:
EMAIL ADDRESS:	WITNESS SIGNATURE:
ADDRESS:	

DOCUMENT TYPE:	DATE/TIME NOTARIZED:	DOCUMENT DATE:	FEE CHARGED:
COMMENTS:			RECORD NUMBER: 36

NOTARY LOG

FULL NAME:	PHONE NUMBER:	THUMB PRINT
EMAIL ADDRESS:	SIGNER'S SIGNATURE	
ADDRESS:		

SERVICE PERFORMED:
- ❑ JURAT
- ❑ OATH
- ❑ ACKNOWLEDGEMENT
- ❑ OTHER: _____

IDENTIFICATION
- ❑ ID CARD
- ❑ PASSPORT
- ❑ DRIVER'S LICENSE
- ❑ OTHER: _____
- ❑ CREDIBLE WITNESS
- ❑ KNOWN PERSONALLY

ID NUMBER:

ISSUED BY:

DATE ISSUED: EXPIRATION DATE:

WITNESS FULL NAME:	PHONE NUMBER:
EMAIL ADDRESS:	WITNESS SIGNATURE:
ADDRESS:	

DOCUMENT TYPE:	DATE/TIME NOTARIZED:	DOCUMENT DATE:	FEE CHARGED:

COMMENTS: RECORD NUMBER: **37**

NOTARY LOG

FULL NAME:	PHONE NUMBER:	THUMB PRINT
EMAIL ADDRESS:	SIGNER'S SIGNATURE	
ADDRESS:		

SERVICE PERFORMED:
- ❑ JURAT
- ❑ OATH
- ❑ ACKNOWLEDGEMENT
- ❑ OTHER: _____

IDENTIFICATION
- ❑ ID CARD
- ❑ PASSPORT
- ❑ DRIVER'S LICENSE
- ❑ OTHER: _____
- ❑ CREDIBLE WITNESS
- ❑ KNOWN PERSONALLY

ID NUMBER:

ISSUED BY:

DATE ISSUED: EXPIRATION DATE:

WITNESS FULL NAME:	PHONE NUMBER:
EMAIL ADDRESS:	WITNESS SIGNATURE:
ADDRESS:	

DOCUMENT TYPE:	DATE/TIME NOTARIZED:	DOCUMENT DATE:	FEE CHARGED:

COMMENTS: RECORD NUMBER: **38**

NOTARY LOG

FULL NAME:	PHONE NUMBER:	THUMB PRINT
EMAIL ADDRESS:	SIGNER'S SIGNATURE	
ADDRESS:		

SERVICE PERFORMED:	IDENTIFICATION	ID NUMBER:
❑ JURAT	❑ ID CARD ❑ CREDIBLE WITNESS	
❑ OATH	❑ PASSPORT ❑ KNOWN PERSONALLY	ISSUED BY:
❑ ACKNOWLEDGEMENT	❑ DRIVER'S LICENSE	
❑ OTHER: _____	❑ OTHER: _____	DATE ISSUED: EXPIRATION DATE:

WITNESS FULL NAME:	PHONE NUMBER:
EMAIL ADDRESS:	WITNESS SIGNATURE:
ADDRESS:	

DOCUMENT TYPE:	DATE/TIME NOTARIZED:	DOCUMENT DATE:	FEE CHARGED:
COMMENTS:			RECORD NUMBER: **39**

NOTARY LOG

FULL NAME:	PHONE NUMBER:	THUMB PRINT
EMAIL ADDRESS:	SIGNER'S SIGNATURE	
ADDRESS:		

SERVICE PERFORMED:	IDENTIFICATION	ID NUMBER:
❑ JURAT	❑ ID CARD ❑ CREDIBLE WITNESS	
❑ OATH	❑ PASSPORT ❑ KNOWN PERSONALLY	ISSUED BY:
❑ ACKNOWLEDGEMENT	❑ DRIVER'S LICENSE	
❑ OTHER: _____	❑ OTHER: _____	DATE ISSUED: EXPIRATION DATE:

WITNESS FULL NAME:	PHONE NUMBER:
EMAIL ADDRESS:	WITNESS SIGNATURE:
ADDRESS:	

DOCUMENT TYPE:	DATE/TIME NOTARIZED:	DOCUMENT DATE:	FEE CHARGED:
COMMENTS:			RECORD NUMBER: **40**

NOTARY LOG

FULL NAME:

PHONE NUMBER:

THUMB PRINT

EMAIL ADDRESS:

SIGNER'S SIGNATURE

ADDRESS:

SERVICE PERFORMED:
- ❑ JURAT
- ❑ OATH
- ❑ ACKNOWLEDGEMENT
- ❑ OTHER: _____

IDENTIFICATION
- ❑ ID CARD
- ❑ PASSPORT
- ❑ DRIVER'S LICENSE
- ❑ OTHER: _____
- ❑ CREDIBLE WITNESS
- ❑ KNOWN PERSONALLY

ID NUMBER:

ISSUED BY:

DATE ISSUED:

EXPIRATION DATE:

WITNESS FULL NAME:

PHONE NUMBER:

EMAIL ADDRESS:

WITNESS SIGNATURE:

ADDRESS:

DOCUMENT TYPE:

DATE/TIME NOTARIZED:

DOCUMENT DATE:

FEE CHARGED:

COMMENTS:

RECORD NUMBER: 41

NOTARY LOG

FULL NAME:

PHONE NUMBER:

THUMB PRINT

EMAIL ADDRESS:

SIGNER'S SIGNATURE

ADDRESS:

SERVICE PERFORMED:
- ❑ JURAT
- ❑ OATH
- ❑ ACKNOWLEDGEMENT
- ❑ OTHER: _____

IDENTIFICATION
- ❑ ID CARD
- ❑ PASSPORT
- ❑ DRIVER'S LICENSE
- ❑ OTHER: _____
- ❑ CREDIBLE WITNESS
- ❑ KNOWN PERSONALLY

ID NUMBER:

ISSUED BY:

DATE ISSUED:

EXPIRATION DATE:

WITNESS FULL NAME:

PHONE NUMBER:

EMAIL ADDRESS:

WITNESS SIGNATURE:

ADDRESS:

DOCUMENT TYPE:

DATE/TIME NOTARIZED:

DOCUMENT DATE:

FEE CHARGED:

COMMENTS:

RECORD NUMBER: 42

NOTARY LOG

FULL NAME:	PHONE NUMBER:	THUMB PRINT
EMAIL ADDRESS:	SIGNER'S SIGNATURE	
ADDRESS:		

SERVICE PERFORMED:	IDENTIFICATION	ID NUMBER:
❑ JURAT	❑ ID CARD ❑ CREDIBLE WITNESS	
❑ OATH	❑ PASSPORT ❑ KNOWN PERSONALLY	ISSUED BY:
❑ ACKNOWLEDGEMENT	❑ DRIVER'S LICENSE	
❑ OTHER: _____	❑ OTHER: _____	DATE ISSUED: EXPIRATION DATE:

WITNESS FULL NAME:	PHONE NUMBER:
EMAIL ADDRESS:	WITNESS SIGNATURE:
ADDRESS:	

DOCUMENT TYPE:	DATE/TIME NOTARIZED:	DOCUMENT DATE:	FEE CHARGED:
COMMENTS:			RECORD NUMBER: **43**

NOTARY LOG

FULL NAME:	PHONE NUMBER:	THUMB PRINT
EMAIL ADDRESS:	SIGNER'S SIGNATURE	
ADDRESS:		

SERVICE PERFORMED:	IDENTIFICATION	ID NUMBER:
❑ JURAT	❑ ID CARD ❑ CREDIBLE WITNESS	
❑ OATH	❑ PASSPORT ❑ KNOWN PERSONALLY	ISSUED BY:
❑ ACKNOWLEDGEMENT	❑ DRIVER'S LICENSE	
❑ OTHER: _____	❑ OTHER: _____	DATE ISSUED: EXPIRATION DATE:

WITNESS FULL NAME:	PHONE NUMBER:
EMAIL ADDRESS:	WITNESS SIGNATURE:
ADDRESS:	

DOCUMENT TYPE:	DATE/TIME NOTARIZED:	DOCUMENT DATE:	FEE CHARGED:
COMMENTS:			RECORD NUMBER: **44**

NOTARY LOG

FULL NAME:	PHONE NUMBER:	THUMB PRINT
EMAIL ADDRESS:	SIGNER'S SIGNATURE	
ADDRESS:		

SERVICE PERFORMED:	IDENTIFICATION	ID NUMBER:
❏ JURAT	❏ ID CARD ❏ CREDIBLE WITNESS	
❏ OATH	❏ PASSPORT ❏ KNOWN PERSONALLY	ISSUED BY:
❏ ACKNOWLEDGEMENT	❏ DRIVER'S LICENSE	
❏ OTHER: _____	❏ OTHER: _____	DATE ISSUED: / EXPIRATION DATE:

WITNESS FULL NAME:	PHONE NUMBER:
EMAIL ADDRESS:	WITNESS SIGNATURE:
ADDRESS:	

DOCUMENT TYPE:	DATE/TIME NOTARIZED:	DOCUMENT DATE:	FEE CHARGED:
COMMENTS:			RECORD NUMBER: **45**

NOTARY LOG

FULL NAME:	PHONE NUMBER:	THUMB PRINT
EMAIL ADDRESS:	SIGNER'S SIGNATURE	
ADDRESS:		

SERVICE PERFORMED:	IDENTIFICATION	ID NUMBER:
❏ JURAT	❏ ID CARD ❏ CREDIBLE WITNESS	
❏ OATH	❏ PASSPORT ❏ KNOWN PERSONALLY	ISSUED BY:
❏ ACKNOWLEDGEMENT	❏ DRIVER'S LICENSE	
❏ OTHER: _____	❏ OTHER: _____	DATE ISSUED: / EXPIRATION DATE:

WITNESS FULL NAME:	PHONE NUMBER:
EMAIL ADDRESS:	WITNESS SIGNATURE:
ADDRESS:	

DOCUMENT TYPE:	DATE/TIME NOTARIZED:	DOCUMENT DATE:	FEE CHARGED:
COMMENTS:			RECORD NUMBER: **46**

NOTARY LOG

FULL NAME:	PHONE NUMBER:	THUMB PRINT
EMAIL ADDRESS:	SIGNER'S SIGNATURE	
ADDRESS:		

SERVICE PERFORMED:
- ❑ JURAT
- ❑ OATH
- ❑ ACKNOWLEDGEMENT
- ❑ OTHER: _____

IDENTIFICATION
- ❑ ID CARD
- ❑ PASSPORT
- ❑ DRIVER'S LICENSE
- ❑ OTHER: _____
- ❑ CREDIBLE WITNESS
- ❑ KNOWN PERSONALLY

ID NUMBER:

ISSUED BY:

DATE ISSUED: EXPIRATION DATE:

WITNESS FULL NAME:	PHONE NUMBER:
EMAIL ADDRESS:	WITNESS SIGNATURE:
ADDRESS:	

DOCUMENT TYPE:	DATE/TIME NOTARIZED:	DOCUMENT DATE:	FEE CHARGED:
COMMENTS:			RECORD NUMBER: **47**

NOTARY LOG

FULL NAME:	PHONE NUMBER:	THUMB PRINT
EMAIL ADDRESS:	SIGNER'S SIGNATURE	
ADDRESS:		

SERVICE PERFORMED:
- ❑ JURAT
- ❑ OATH
- ❑ ACKNOWLEDGEMENT
- ❑ OTHER: _____

IDENTIFICATION
- ❑ ID CARD
- ❑ PASSPORT
- ❑ DRIVER'S LICENSE
- ❑ OTHER: _____
- ❑ CREDIBLE WITNESS
- ❑ KNOWN PERSONALLY

ID NUMBER:

ISSUED BY:

DATE ISSUED: EXPIRATION DATE:

WITNESS FULL NAME:	PHONE NUMBER:
EMAIL ADDRESS:	WITNESS SIGNATURE:
ADDRESS:	

DOCUMENT TYPE:	DATE/TIME NOTARIZED:	DOCUMENT DATE:	FEE CHARGED:
COMMENTS:			RECORD NUMBER: **48**

NOTARY LOG

FULL NAME:	PHONE NUMBER:	THUMB PRINT
EMAIL ADDRESS:	SIGNER'S SIGNATURE	
ADDRESS:		

SERVICE PERFORMED:
- ❑ JURAT
- ❑ OATH
- ❑ ACKNOWLEDGEMENT
- ❑ OTHER: _____

IDENTIFICATION
- ❑ ID CARD
- ❑ PASSPORT
- ❑ DRIVER'S LICENSE
- ❑ OTHER: _____
- ❑ CREDIBLE WITNESS
- ❑ KNOWN PERSONALLY

ID NUMBER:

ISSUED BY:

DATE ISSUED:	EXPIRATION DATE:

WITNESS FULL NAME:	PHONE NUMBER:
EMAIL ADDRESS:	WITNESS SIGNATURE:
ADDRESS:	

DOCUMENT TYPE:	DATE/TIME NOTARIZED:	DOCUMENT DATE:	FEE CHARGED:

COMMENTS:		RECORD NUMBER: 49

NOTARY LOG

FULL NAME:	PHONE NUMBER:	THUMB PRINT
EMAIL ADDRESS:	SIGNER'S SIGNATURE	
ADDRESS:		

SERVICE PERFORMED:
- ❑ JURAT
- ❑ OATH
- ❑ ACKNOWLEDGEMENT
- ❑ OTHER: _____

IDENTIFICATION
- ❑ ID CARD
- ❑ PASSPORT
- ❑ DRIVER'S LICENSE
- ❑ OTHER: _____
- ❑ CREDIBLE WITNESS
- ❑ KNOWN PERSONALLY

ID NUMBER:

ISSUED BY:

DATE ISSUED:	EXPIRATION DATE:

WITNESS FULL NAME:	PHONE NUMBER:
EMAIL ADDRESS:	WITNESS SIGNATURE:
ADDRESS:	

DOCUMENT TYPE:	DATE/TIME NOTARIZED:	DOCUMENT DATE:	FEE CHARGED:

COMMENTS:		RECORD NUMBER: 50

NOTARY LOG

FULL NAME:	PHONE NUMBER:	THUMB PRINT
EMAIL ADDRESS:	SIGNER'S SIGNATURE	
ADDRESS:		

SERVICE PERFORMED:	IDENTIFICATION	ID NUMBER:
❑ JURAT	❑ ID CARD ❑ CREDIBLE WITNESS	
❑ OATH	❑ PASSPORT ❑ KNOWN PERSONALLY	ISSUED BY:
❑ ACKNOWLEDGEMENT	❑ DRIVER'S LICENSE	
❑ OTHER: _____	❑ OTHER: _____	DATE ISSUED: EXPIRATION DATE:

WITNESS FULL NAME:	PHONE NUMBER:
EMAIL ADDRESS:	WITNESS SIGNATURE:
ADDRESS:	

DOCUMENT TYPE:	DATE/TIME NOTARIZED:	DOCUMENT DATE:	FEE CHARGED:
COMMENTS:			RECORD NUMBER: 51

NOTARY LOG

FULL NAME:	PHONE NUMBER:	THUMB PRINT
EMAIL ADDRESS:	SIGNER'S SIGNATURE	
ADDRESS:		

SERVICE PERFORMED:	IDENTIFICATION	ID NUMBER:
❑ JURAT	❑ ID CARD ❑ CREDIBLE WITNESS	
❑ OATH	❑ PASSPORT ❑ KNOWN PERSONALLY	ISSUED BY:
❑ ACKNOWLEDGEMENT	❑ DRIVER'S LICENSE	
❑ OTHER: _____	❑ OTHER: _____	DATE ISSUED: EXPIRATION DATE:

WITNESS FULL NAME:	PHONE NUMBER:
EMAIL ADDRESS:	WITNESS SIGNATURE:
ADDRESS:	

DOCUMENT TYPE:	DATE/TIME NOTARIZED:	DOCUMENT DATE:	FEE CHARGED:
COMMENTS:			RECORD NUMBER: 52

NOTARY LOG

FULL NAME:	PHONE NUMBER:	THUMB PRINT
EMAIL ADDRESS:	SIGNER'S SIGNATURE	
ADDRESS:		

SERVICE PERFORMED:
- ❏ JURAT
- ❏ OATH
- ❏ ACKNOWLEDGEMENT
- ❏ OTHER: _____

IDENTIFICATION
- ❏ ID CARD
- ❏ PASSPORT
- ❏ DRIVER'S LICENSE
- ❏ OTHER: _____
- ❏ CREDIBLE WITNESS
- ❏ KNOWN PERSONALLY

ID NUMBER:

ISSUED BY:

DATE ISSUED:	EXPIRATION DATE:

WITNESS FULL NAME:	PHONE NUMBER:
EMAIL ADDRESS:	WITNESS SIGNATURE:
ADDRESS:	

DOCUMENT TYPE:	DATE/TIME NOTARIZED:	DOCUMENT DATE:	FEE CHARGED:

COMMENTS:		RECORD NUMBER: 53

NOTARY LOG

FULL NAME:	PHONE NUMBER:	THUMB PRINT
EMAIL ADDRESS:	SIGNER'S SIGNATURE	
ADDRESS:		

SERVICE PERFORMED:
- ❏ JURAT
- ❏ OATH
- ❏ ACKNOWLEDGEMENT
- ❏ OTHER: _____

IDENTIFICATION
- ❏ ID CARD
- ❏ PASSPORT
- ❏ DRIVER'S LICENSE
- ❏ OTHER: _____
- ❏ CREDIBLE WITNESS
- ❏ KNOWN PERSONALLY

ID NUMBER:

ISSUED BY:

DATE ISSUED:	EXPIRATION DATE:

WITNESS FULL NAME:	PHONE NUMBER:
EMAIL ADDRESS:	WITNESS SIGNATURE:
ADDRESS:	

DOCUMENT TYPE:	DATE/TIME NOTARIZED:	DOCUMENT DATE:	FEE CHARGED:

COMMENTS:		RECORD NUMBER: 54

NOTARY LOG

FULL NAME:	PHONE NUMBER:	THUMB PRINT
EMAIL ADDRESS:	SIGNER'S SIGNATURE	
ADDRESS:		

SERVICE PERFORMED:	IDENTIFICATION		ID NUMBER:
❑ JURAT	❑ ID CARD	❑ CREDIBLE WITNESS	
❑ OATH	❑ PASSPORT	❑ KNOWN PERSONALLY	ISSUED BY:
❑ ACKNOWLEDGEMENT	❑ DRIVER'S LICENSE		
❑ OTHER: _____	❑ OTHER: _____		DATE ISSUED: / EXPIRATION DATE:

WITNESS FULL NAME:	PHONE NUMBER:
EMAIL ADDRESS:	WITNESS SIGNATURE:
ADDRESS:	

DOCUMENT TYPE:	DATE/TIME NOTARIZED:	DOCUMENT DATE:	FEE CHARGED:
COMMENTS:			RECORD NUMBER: **55**

NOTARY LOG

FULL NAME:	PHONE NUMBER:	THUMB PRINT
EMAIL ADDRESS:	SIGNER'S SIGNATURE	
ADDRESS:		

SERVICE PERFORMED:	IDENTIFICATION		ID NUMBER:
❑ JURAT	❑ ID CARD	❑ CREDIBLE WITNESS	
❑ OATH	❑ PASSPORT	❑ KNOWN PERSONALLY	ISSUED BY:
❑ ACKNOWLEDGEMENT	❑ DRIVER'S LICENSE		
❑ OTHER: _____	❑ OTHER: _____		DATE ISSUED: / EXPIRATION DATE:

WITNESS FULL NAME:	PHONE NUMBER:
EMAIL ADDRESS:	WITNESS SIGNATURE:
ADDRESS:	

DOCUMENT TYPE:	DATE/TIME NOTARIZED:	DOCUMENT DATE:	FEE CHARGED:
COMMENTS:			RECORD NUMBER: **56**

NOTARY LOG

		THUMB PRINT
FULL NAME:	**PHONE NUMBER:**	
EMAIL ADDRESS:	**SIGNER'S SIGNATURE**	
ADDRESS:		

SERVICE PERFORMED:

- ❏ JURAT
- ❏ OATH
- ❏ ACKNOWLEDGEMENT
- ❏ OTHER: _____

IDENTIFICATION

- ❏ ID CARD
- ❏ PASSPORT
- ❏ DRIVER'S LICENSE
- ❏ OTHER: _____
- ❏ CREDIBLE WITNESS
- ❏ KNOWN PERSONALLY

ID NUMBER:

ISSUED BY:

DATE ISSUED: **EXPIRATION DATE:**

WITNESS FULL NAME:	**PHONE NUMBER:**
EMAIL ADDRESS:	**WITNESS SIGNATURE:**
ADDRESS:	

DOCUMENT TYPE:	**DATE/TIME NOTARIZED:**	**DOCUMENT DATE:**	**FEE CHARGED:**

COMMENTS:

RECORD NUMBER: 57

NOTARY LOG

		THUMB PRINT
FULL NAME:	**PHONE NUMBER:**	
EMAIL ADDRESS:	**SIGNER'S SIGNATURE**	
ADDRESS:		

SERVICE PERFORMED:

- ❏ JURAT
- ❏ OATH
- ❏ ACKNOWLEDGEMENT
- ❏ OTHER: _____

IDENTIFICATION

- ❏ ID CARD
- ❏ PASSPORT
- ❏ DRIVER'S LICENSE
- ❏ OTHER: _____
- ❏ CREDIBLE WITNESS
- ❏ KNOWN PERSONALLY

ID NUMBER:

ISSUED BY:

DATE ISSUED: **EXPIRATION DATE:**

WITNESS FULL NAME:	**PHONE NUMBER:**
EMAIL ADDRESS:	**WITNESS SIGNATURE:**
ADDRESS:	

DOCUMENT TYPE:	**DATE/TIME NOTARIZED:**	**DOCUMENT DATE:**	**FEE CHARGED:**

COMMENTS:

RECORD NUMBER: 58

NOTARY LOG

FULL NAME:	PHONE NUMBER:	THUMB PRINT
EMAIL ADDRESS:	SIGNER'S SIGNATURE	
ADDRESS:		

SERVICE PERFORMED:	IDENTIFICATION	ID NUMBER:
❑ JURAT	❑ ID CARD ❑ CREDIBLE WITNESS	
❑ OATH	❑ PASSPORT ❑ KNOWN PERSONALLY	ISSUED BY:
❑ ACKNOWLEDGEMENT	❑ DRIVER'S LICENSE	
❑ OTHER: _____	❑ OTHER: _____	DATE ISSUED:	EXPIRATION DATE:

WITNESS FULL NAME:	PHONE NUMBER:
EMAIL ADDRESS:	WITNESS SIGNATURE:
ADDRESS:	

DOCUMENT TYPE:	DATE/TIME NOTARIZED:	DOCUMENT DATE:	FEE CHARGED:
COMMENTS:			RECORD NUMBER: **59**

NOTARY LOG

FULL NAME:	PHONE NUMBER:	THUMB PRINT
EMAIL ADDRESS:	SIGNER'S SIGNATURE	
ADDRESS:		

SERVICE PERFORMED:	IDENTIFICATION	ID NUMBER:
❑ JURAT	❑ ID CARD ❑ CREDIBLE WITNESS	
❑ OATH	❑ PASSPORT ❑ KNOWN PERSONALLY	ISSUED BY:
❑ ACKNOWLEDGEMENT	❑ DRIVER'S LICENSE	
❑ OTHER: _____	❑ OTHER: _____	DATE ISSUED:	EXPIRATION DATE:

WITNESS FULL NAME:	PHONE NUMBER:
EMAIL ADDRESS:	WITNESS SIGNATURE:
ADDRESS:	

DOCUMENT TYPE:	DATE/TIME NOTARIZED:	DOCUMENT DATE:	FEE CHARGED:
COMMENTS:			RECORD NUMBER: **60**

NOTARY LOG

FULL NAME:	PHONE NUMBER:	THUMB PRINT
EMAIL ADDRESS:	SIGNER'S SIGNATURE	
ADDRESS:		

SERVICE PERFORMED:
- ☐ JURAT
- ☐ OATH
- ☐ ACKNOWLEDGEMENT
- ☐ OTHER: _____

IDENTIFICATION
- ☐ ID CARD
- ☐ PASSPORT
- ☐ DRIVER'S LICENSE
- ☐ OTHER: _____
- ☐ CREDIBLE WITNESS
- ☐ KNOWN PERSONALLY

ID NUMBER:

ISSUED BY:

DATE ISSUED:	EXPIRATION DATE:

WITNESS FULL NAME:	PHONE NUMBER:
EMAIL ADDRESS:	WITNESS SIGNATURE:
ADDRESS:	

DOCUMENT TYPE:	DATE/TIME NOTARIZED:	DOCUMENT DATE:	FEE CHARGED:

COMMENTS:		RECORD NUMBER: 61

NOTARY LOG

FULL NAME:	PHONE NUMBER:	THUMB PRINT
EMAIL ADDRESS:	SIGNER'S SIGNATURE	
ADDRESS:		

SERVICE PERFORMED:
- ☐ JURAT
- ☐ OATH
- ☐ ACKNOWLEDGEMENT
- ☐ OTHER: _____

IDENTIFICATION
- ☐ ID CARD
- ☐ PASSPORT
- ☐ DRIVER'S LICENSE
- ☐ OTHER: _____
- ☐ CREDIBLE WITNESS
- ☐ KNOWN PERSONALLY

ID NUMBER:

ISSUED BY:

DATE ISSUED:	EXPIRATION DATE:

WITNESS FULL NAME:	PHONE NUMBER:
EMAIL ADDRESS:	WITNESS SIGNATURE:
ADDRESS:	

DOCUMENT TYPE:	DATE/TIME NOTARIZED:	DOCUMENT DATE:	FEE CHARGED:

COMMENTS:		RECORD NUMBER: 62

NOTARY LOG

FULL NAME:	PHONE NUMBER:	THUMB PRINT
EMAIL ADDRESS:	SIGNER'S SIGNATURE	
ADDRESS:		

SERVICE PERFORMED:	IDENTIFICATION	ID NUMBER:
❑ JURAT	❑ ID CARD ❑ CREDIBLE WITNESS	
❑ OATH	❑ PASSPORT ❑ KNOWN PERSONALLY	ISSUED BY:
❑ ACKNOWLEDGEMENT	❑ DRIVER'S LICENSE	
❑ OTHER: _____	❑ OTHER: _____	DATE ISSUED: EXPIRATION DATE:

WITNESS FULL NAME:	PHONE NUMBER:
EMAIL ADDRESS:	WITNESS SIGNATURE
ADDRESS:	

DOCUMENT TYPE:	DATE/TIME NOTARIZED:	DOCUMENT DATE:	FEE CHARGED:
COMMENTS:			RECORD NUMBER: 63

NOTARY LOG

FULL NAME:	PHONE NUMBER:	THUMB PRINT
EMAIL ADDRESS:	SIGNER'S SIGNATURE	
ADDRESS:		

SERVICE PERFORMED:	IDENTIFICATION	ID NUMBER:
❑ JURAT	❑ ID CARD ❑ CREDIBLE WITNESS	
❑ OATH	❑ PASSPORT ❑ KNOWN PERSONALLY	ISSUED BY:
❑ ACKNOWLEDGEMENT	❑ DRIVER'S LICENSE	
❑ OTHER: _____	❑ OTHER: _____	DATE ISSUED: EXPIRATION DATE:

WITNESS FULL NAME:	PHONE NUMBER:
EMAIL ADDRESS:	WITNESS SIGNATURE
ADDRESS:	

DOCUMENT TYPE:	DATE/TIME NOTARIZED:	DOCUMENT DATE:	FEE CHARGED:
COMMENTS:			RECORD NUMBER: 64

NOTARY LOG

FULL NAME:	PHONE NUMBER:	THUMB PRINT
EMAIL ADDRESS:	SIGNER'S SIGNATURE	
ADDRESS:		

SERVICE PERFORMED:
- ❑ JURAT
- ❑ OATH
- ❑ ACKNOWLEDGEMENT
- ❑ OTHER: _____

IDENTIFICATION
- ❑ ID CARD
- ❑ PASSPORT
- ❑ DRIVER'S LICENSE
- ❑ OTHER: _____
- ❑ CREDIBLE WITNESS
- ❑ KNOWN PERSONALLY

ID NUMBER:

ISSUED BY:

DATE ISSUED: EXPIRATION DATE:

WITNESS FULL NAME:	PHONE NUMBER:
EMAIL ADDRESS:	WITNESS SIGNATURE:
ADDRESS:	

DOCUMENT TYPE:	DATE/TIME NOTARIZED:	DOCUMENT DATE:	FEE CHARGED:

COMMENTS: RECORD NUMBER: **65**

NOTARY LOG

FULL NAME:	PHONE NUMBER:	THUMB PRINT
EMAIL ADDRESS:	SIGNER'S SIGNATURE	
ADDRESS:		

SERVICE PERFORMED:
- ❑ JURAT
- ❑ OATH
- ❑ ACKNOWLEDGEMENT
- ❑ OTHER: _____

IDENTIFICATION
- ❑ ID CARD
- ❑ PASSPORT
- ❑ DRIVER'S LICENSE
- ❑ OTHER: _____
- ❑ CREDIBLE WITNESS
- ❑ KNOWN PERSONALLY

ID NUMBER:

ISSUED BY:

DATE ISSUED: EXPIRATION DATE:

WITNESS FULL NAME:	PHONE NUMBER:
EMAIL ADDRESS:	WITNESS SIGNATURE:
ADDRESS:	

DOCUMENT TYPE:	DATE/TIME NOTARIZED:	DOCUMENT DATE:	FEE CHARGED:

COMMENTS: RECORD NUMBER: **66**

NOTARY LOG

FULL NAME:	PHONE NUMBER:	THUMB PRINT
EMAIL ADDRESS:	SIGNER'S SIGNATURE	
ADDRESS:		

SERVICE PERFORMED:	IDENTIFICATION	ID NUMBER:
❏ JURAT	❏ ID CARD ❏ CREDIBLE WITNESS	
❏ OATH	❏ PASSPORT ❏ KNOWN PERSONALLY	ISSUED BY:
❏ ACKNOWLEDGEMENT	❏ DRIVER'S LICENSE	
❏ OTHER: _____	❏ OTHER: _____	DATE ISSUED: / EXPIRATION DATE:

WITNESS FULL NAME:	PHONE NUMBER:
EMAIL ADDRESS:	WITNESS SIGNATURE
ADDRESS:	

DOCUMENT TYPE:	DATE/TIME NOTARIZED:	DOCUMENT DATE:	FEE CHARGED:
COMMENTS:		RECORD NUMBER:	67

NOTARY LOG

FULL NAME:	PHONE NUMBER:	THUMB PRINT
EMAIL ADDRESS:	SIGNER'S SIGNATURE	
ADDRESS:		

SERVICE PERFORMED:	IDENTIFICATION	ID NUMBER:
❏ JURAT	❏ ID CARD ❏ CREDIBLE WITNESS	
❏ OATH	❏ PASSPORT ❏ KNOWN PERSONALLY	ISSUED BY:
❏ ACKNOWLEDGEMENT	❏ DRIVER'S LICENSE	
❏ OTHER: _____	❏ OTHER: _____	DATE ISSUED: / EXPIRATION DATE:

WITNESS FULL NAME:	PHONE NUMBER:
EMAIL ADDRESS:	WITNESS SIGNATURE
ADDRESS:	

DOCUMENT TYPE:	DATE/TIME NOTARIZED:	DOCUMENT DATE:	FEE CHARGED:
COMMENTS:		RECORD NUMBER:	68

NOTARY LOG

FULL NAME:	PHONE NUMBER:	THUMB PRINT
EMAIL ADDRESS:	SIGNER'S SIGNATURE	
ADDRESS:		

SERVICE PERFORMED:	IDENTIFICATION	ID NUMBER:
❑ JURAT	❑ ID CARD ❑ CREDIBLE WITNESS	
❑ OATH	❑ PASSPORT ❑ KNOWN PERSONALLY	ISSUED BY:
❑ ACKNOWLEDGEMENT	❑ DRIVER'S LICENSE	
❑ OTHER: _____	❑ OTHER: _____	DATE ISSUED: / EXPIRATION DATE:

WITNESS FULL NAME:	PHONE NUMBER:
EMAIL ADDRESS:	WITNESS SIGNATURE:
ADDRESS:	

DOCUMENT TYPE:	DATE/TIME NOTARIZED:	DOCUMENT DATE:	FEE CHARGED:
COMMENTS:			RECORD NUMBER: **69**

NOTARY LOG

FULL NAME:	PHONE NUMBER:	THUMB PRINT
EMAIL ADDRESS:	SIGNER'S SIGNATURE	
ADDRESS:		

SERVICE PERFORMED:	IDENTIFICATION	ID NUMBER:
❑ JURAT	❑ ID CARD ❑ CREDIBLE WITNESS	
❑ OATH	❑ PASSPORT ❑ KNOWN PERSONALLY	ISSUED BY:
❑ ACKNOWLEDGEMENT	❑ DRIVER'S LICENSE	
❑ OTHER: _____	❑ OTHER: _____	DATE ISSUED: / EXPIRATION DATE:

WITNESS FULL NAME:	PHONE NUMBER:
EMAIL ADDRESS:	WITNESS SIGNATURE:
ADDRESS:	

DOCUMENT TYPE:	DATE/TIME NOTARIZED:	DOCUMENT DATE:	FEE CHARGED:
COMMENTS:			RECORD NUMBER: **70**

NOTARY LOG

FULL NAME:	PHONE NUMBER:	THUMB PRINT
EMAIL ADDRESS:	SIGNER'S SIGNATURE	
ADDRESS:		

SERVICE PERFORMED:
- ❑ JURAT
- ❑ OATH
- ❑ ACKNOWLEDGEMENT
- ❑ OTHER: _____

IDENTIFICATION
- ❑ ID CARD
- ❑ PASSPORT
- ❑ DRIVER'S LICENSE
- ❑ OTHER: _____
- ❑ CREDIBLE WITNESS
- ❑ KNOWN PERSONALLY

ID NUMBER:

ISSUED BY:

DATE ISSUED:

EXPIRATION DATE:

WITNESS FULL NAME:	PHONE NUMBER:
EMAIL ADDRESS:	WITNESS SIGNATURE:
ADDRESS:	

DOCUMENT TYPE:	DATE/TIME NOTARIZED:	DOCUMENT DATE:	FEE CHARGED:
COMMENTS:		RECORD NUMBER:	71

NOTARY LOG

FULL NAME:	PHONE NUMBER:	THUMB PRINT
EMAIL ADDRESS:	SIGNER'S SIGNATURE	
ADDRESS:		

SERVICE PERFORMED:
- ❑ JURAT
- ❑ OATH
- ❑ ACKNOWLEDGEMENT
- ❑ OTHER: _____

IDENTIFICATION
- ❑ ID CARD
- ❑ PASSPORT
- ❑ DRIVER'S LICENSE
- ❑ OTHER: _____
- ❑ CREDIBLE WITNESS
- ❑ KNOWN PERSONALLY

ID NUMBER:

ISSUED BY:

DATE ISSUED:

EXPIRATION DATE:

WITNESS FULL NAME:	PHONE NUMBER:
EMAIL ADDRESS:	WITNESS SIGNATURE:
ADDRESS:	

DOCUMENT TYPE:	DATE/TIME NOTARIZED:	DOCUMENT DATE:	FEE CHARGED:
COMMENTS:		RECORD NUMBER:	72

NOTARY LOG

FULL NAME:	PHONE NUMBER:	THUMB PRINT
EMAIL ADDRESS:	SIGNER'S SIGNATURE	
ADDRESS:		

SERVICE PERFORMED:	IDENTIFICATION	ID NUMBER:
❑ JURAT	❑ ID CARD ❑ CREDIBLE WITNESS	
❑ OATH	❑ PASSPORT ❑ KNOWN PERSONALLY	ISSUED BY:
❑ ACKNOWLEDGEMENT	❑ DRIVER'S LICENSE	DATE ISSUED: EXPIRATION DATE:
❑ OTHER: _____	❑ OTHER: _____	

WITNESS FULL NAME:	PHONE NUMBER:
EMAIL ADDRESS:	WITNESS SIGNATURE:
ADDRESS:	

DOCUMENT TYPE:	DATE/TIME NOTARIZED:	DOCUMENT DATE:	FEE CHARGED:
COMMENTS:			RECORD NUMBER: 73

NOTARY LOG

FULL NAME:	PHONE NUMBER:	THUMB PRINT
EMAIL ADDRESS:	SIGNER'S SIGNATURE	
ADDRESS:		

SERVICE PERFORMED:	IDENTIFICATION	ID NUMBER:
❑ JURAT	❑ ID CARD ❑ CREDIBLE WITNESS	
❑ OATH	❑ PASSPORT ❑ KNOWN PERSONALLY	ISSUED BY:
❑ ACKNOWLEDGEMENT	❑ DRIVER'S LICENSE	DATE ISSUED: EXPIRATION DATE:
❑ OTHER: _____	❑ OTHER: _____	

WITNESS FULL NAME:	PHONE NUMBER:
EMAIL ADDRESS:	WITNESS SIGNATURE:
ADDRESS:	

DOCUMENT TYPE:	DATE/TIME NOTARIZED:	DOCUMENT DATE:	FEE CHARGED:
COMMENTS:			RECORD NUMBER: 74

NOTARY LOG

FULL NAME:	PHONE NUMBER:	THUMB PRINT

EMAIL ADDRESS:

ADDRESS:

SIGNER'S SIGNATURE

SERVICE PERFORMED:	IDENTIFICATION	ID NUMBER:

SERVICE PERFORMED:
- ❑ JURAT
- ❑ OATH
- ❑ ACKNOWLEDGEMENT
- ❑ OTHER: _____

IDENTIFICATION
- ❑ ID CARD
- ❑ PASSPORT
- ❑ DRIVER'S LICENSE
- ❑ OTHER: _____
- ❑ CREDIBLE WITNESS
- ❑ KNOWN PERSONALLY

ISSUED BY:

DATE ISSUED:	EXPIRATION DATE:

WITNESS FULL NAME: **PHONE NUMBER:**

EMAIL ADDRESS:

ADDRESS:

WITNESS SIGNATURE:

DOCUMENT TYPE:	DATE/TIME NOTARIZED:	DOCUMENT DATE:	FEE CHARGED:

COMMENTS:		RECORD NUMBER:	75

NOTARY LOG

FULL NAME:	PHONE NUMBER:	THUMB PRINT

EMAIL ADDRESS:

ADDRESS:

SIGNER'S SIGNATURE

SERVICE PERFORMED:	IDENTIFICATION	ID NUMBER:

SERVICE PERFORMED:
- ❑ JURAT
- ❑ OATH
- ❑ ACKNOWLEDGEMENT
- ❑ OTHER: _____

IDENTIFICATION
- ❑ ID CARD
- ❑ PASSPORT
- ❑ DRIVER'S LICENSE
- ❑ OTHER: _____
- ❑ CREDIBLE WITNESS
- ❑ KNOWN PERSONALLY

ISSUED BY:

DATE ISSUED:	EXPIRATION DATE:

WITNESS FULL NAME: **PHONE NUMBER:**

EMAIL ADDRESS:

ADDRESS:

WITNESS SIGNATURE:

DOCUMENT TYPE:	DATE/TIME NOTARIZED:	DOCUMENT DATE:	FEE CHARGED:

COMMENTS:		RECORD NUMBER:	76

NOTARY LOG

FULL NAME:

PHONE NUMBER:

THUMB PRINT

EMAIL ADDRESS:

SIGNER'S SIGNATURE

ADDRESS:

SERVICE PERFORMED:
- ❑ JURAT
- ❑ OATH
- ❑ ACKNOWLEDGEMENT
- ❑ OTHER: _____

IDENTIFICATION
- ❑ ID CARD
- ❑ PASSPORT
- ❑ DRIVER'S LICENSE
- ❑ OTHER: _____
- ❑ CREDIBLE WITNESS
- ❑ KNOWN PERSONALLY

ID NUMBER:

ISSUED BY:

DATE ISSUED:

EXPIRATION DATE:

WITNESS FULL NAME:

PHONE NUMBER:

EMAIL ADDRESS:

WITNESS SIGNATURE:

ADDRESS:

DOCUMENT TYPE:	DATE/TIME NOTARIZED:	DOCUMENT DATE:	FEE CHARGED:

COMMENTS:

RECORD NUMBER: 77

NOTARY LOG

FULL NAME:

PHONE NUMBER:

THUMB PRINT

EMAIL ADDRESS:

SIGNER'S SIGNATURE

ADDRESS:

SERVICE PERFORMED:
- ❑ JURAT
- ❑ OATH
- ❑ ACKNOWLEDGEMENT
- ❑ OTHER: _____

IDENTIFICATION
- ❑ ID CARD
- ❑ PASSPORT
- ❑ DRIVER'S LICENSE
- ❑ OTHER: _____
- ❑ CREDIBLE WITNESS
- ❑ KNOWN PERSONALLY

ID NUMBER:

ISSUED BY:

DATE ISSUED:

EXPIRATION DATE:

WITNESS FULL NAME:

PHONE NUMBER:

EMAIL ADDRESS:

WITNESS SIGNATURE:

ADDRESS:

DOCUMENT TYPE:	DATE/TIME NOTARIZED:	DOCUMENT DATE:	FEE CHARGED:

COMMENTS:

RECORD NUMBER: 78

NOTARY LOG

FULL NAME:	PHONE NUMBER:	THUMB PRINT

EMAIL ADDRESS:	SIGNER'S SIGNATURE
ADDRESS:	

SERVICE PERFORMED:
- ❏ JURAT
- ❏ OATH
- ❏ ACKNOWLEDGEMENT
- ❏ OTHER: _____

IDENTIFICATION
- ❏ ID CARD
- ❏ PASSPORT
- ❏ DRIVER'S LICENSE
- ❏ OTHER: _____
- ❏ CREDIBLE WITNESS
- ❏ KNOWN PERSONALLY

ID NUMBER:

ISSUED BY:

DATE ISSUED:	EXPIRATION DATE:

WITNESS FULL NAME:	PHONE NUMBER:
EMAIL ADDRESS:	WITNESS SIGNATURE:
ADDRESS:	

DOCUMENT TYPE:	DATE/TIME NOTARIZED:	DOCUMENT DATE:	FEE CHARGED:

COMMENTS:		RECORD NUMBER: 79

NOTARY LOG

FULL NAME:	PHONE NUMBER:	THUMB PRINT

EMAIL ADDRESS:	SIGNER'S SIGNATURE
ADDRESS:	

SERVICE PERFORMED:
- ❏ JURAT
- ❏ OATH
- ❏ ACKNOWLEDGEMENT
- ❏ OTHER: _____

IDENTIFICATION
- ❏ ID CARD
- ❏ PASSPORT
- ❏ DRIVER'S LICENSE
- ❏ OTHER: _____
- ❏ CREDIBLE WITNESS
- ❏ KNOWN PERSONALLY

ID NUMBER:

ISSUED BY:

DATE ISSUED:	EXPIRATION DATE:

WITNESS FULL NAME:	PHONE NUMBER:
EMAIL ADDRESS:	WITNESS SIGNATURE:
ADDRESS:	

DOCUMENT TYPE:	DATE/TIME NOTARIZED:	DOCUMENT DATE:	FEE CHARGED:

COMMENTS:		RECORD NUMBER: 80

NOTARY LOG

FULL NAME:	PHONE NUMBER:	THUMB PRINT
EMAIL ADDRESS:	SIGNER'S SIGNATURE	
ADDRESS:		

SERVICE PERFORMED:	IDENTIFICATION	ID NUMBER:
❑ JURAT	❑ ID CARD ❑ CREDIBLE WITNESS	
❑ OATH	❑ PASSPORT ❑ KNOWN PERSONALLY	ISSUED BY:
❑ ACKNOWLEDGEMENT	❑ DRIVER'S LICENSE	
❑ OTHER: _____	❑ OTHER: _____	DATE ISSUED: / EXPIRATION DATE:

WITNESS FULL NAME:	PHONE NUMBER:
EMAIL ADDRESS:	WITNESS SIGNATURE:
ADDRESS:	

DOCUMENT TYPE:	DATE/TIME NOTARIZED:	DOCUMENT DATE:	FEE CHARGED:

COMMENTS:		RECORD NUMBER: 81

NOTARY LOG

FULL NAME:	PHONE NUMBER:	THUMB PRINT
EMAIL ADDRESS:	SIGNER'S SIGNATURE	
ADDRESS:		

SERVICE PERFORMED:	IDENTIFICATION	ID NUMBER:
❑ JURAT	❑ ID CARD ❑ CREDIBLE WITNESS	
❑ OATH	❑ PASSPORT ❑ KNOWN PERSONALLY	ISSUED BY:
❑ ACKNOWLEDGEMENT	❑ DRIVER'S LICENSE	
❑ OTHER: _____	❑ OTHER: _____	DATE ISSUED: / EXPIRATION DATE:

WITNESS FULL NAME:	PHONE NUMBER:
EMAIL ADDRESS:	WITNESS SIGNATURE:
ADDRESS:	

DOCUMENT TYPE:	DATE/TIME NOTARIZED:	DOCUMENT DATE:	FEE CHARGED:

COMMENTS:		RECORD NUMBER: 82

NOTARY LOG

		THUMB PRINT
FULL NAME:	**PHONE NUMBER:**	
EMAIL ADDRESS:	**SIGNER'S SIGNATURE**	
ADDRESS:		

SERVICE PERFORMED:	IDENTIFICATION	ID NUMBER:
❑ JURAT	❑ ID CARD ❑ CREDIBLE WITNESS	
❑ OATH	❑ PASSPORT ❑ KNOWN PERSONALLY	ISSUED BY:
❑ ACKNOWLEDGEMENT	❑ DRIVER'S LICENSE	
❑ OTHER: _____	❑ OTHER: _____	DATE ISSUED: | EXPIRATION DATE:

WITNESS FULL NAME:	**PHONE NUMBER:**
EMAIL ADDRESS:	**WITNESS SIGNATURE:**
ADDRESS:	

DOCUMENT TYPE:	DATE/TIME NOTARIZED:	DOCUMENT DATE:	FEE CHARGED:
COMMENTS:			RECORD NUMBER: **83**

NOTARY LOG

		THUMB PRINT
FULL NAME:	**PHONE NUMBER:**	
EMAIL ADDRESS:	**SIGNER'S SIGNATURE**	
ADDRESS:		

SERVICE PERFORMED:	IDENTIFICATION	ID NUMBER:
❑ JURAT	❑ ID CARD ❑ CREDIBLE WITNESS	
❑ OATH	❑ PASSPORT ❑ KNOWN PERSONALLY	ISSUED BY:
❑ ACKNOWLEDGEMENT	❑ DRIVER'S LICENSE	
❑ OTHER: _____	❑ OTHER: _____	DATE ISSUED: | EXPIRATION DATE:

WITNESS FULL NAME:	**PHONE NUMBER:**
EMAIL ADDRESS:	**WITNESS SIGNATURE:**
ADDRESS:	

DOCUMENT TYPE:	DATE/TIME NOTARIZED:	DOCUMENT DATE:	FEE CHARGED:
COMMENTS:			RECORD NUMBER: **84**

NOTARY LOG

FULL NAME:	PHONE NUMBER:	THUMB PRINT
EMAIL ADDRESS:	SIGNER'S SIGNATURE	
ADDRESS:		

SERVICE PERFORMED:
- ❑ JURAT
- ❑ OATH
- ❑ ACKNOWLEDGEMENT
- ❑ OTHER: _____

IDENTIFICATION
- ❑ ID CARD
- ❑ PASSPORT
- ❑ DRIVER'S LICENSE
- ❑ OTHER: _____
- ❑ CREDIBLE WITNESS
- ❑ KNOWN PERSONALLY

ID NUMBER:

ISSUED BY:

DATE ISSUED: EXPIRATION DATE:

WITNESS FULL NAME:	PHONE NUMBER:
EMAIL ADDRESS:	WITNESS SIGNATURE:
ADDRESS:	

DOCUMENT TYPE:	DATE/TIME NOTARIZED:	DOCUMENT DATE:	FEE CHARGED:

COMMENTS:	RECORD NUMBER: **85**

NOTARY LOG

FULL NAME:	PHONE NUMBER:	THUMB PRINT
EMAIL ADDRESS:	SIGNER'S SIGNATURE	
ADDRESS:		

SERVICE PERFORMED:
- ❑ JURAT
- ❑ OATH
- ❑ ACKNOWLEDGEMENT
- ❑ OTHER: _____

IDENTIFICATION
- ❑ ID CARD
- ❑ PASSPORT
- ❑ DRIVER'S LICENSE
- ❑ OTHER: _____
- ❑ CREDIBLE WITNESS
- ❑ KNOWN PERSONALLY

ID NUMBER:

ISSUED BY:

DATE ISSUED: EXPIRATION DATE:

WITNESS FULL NAME:	PHONE NUMBER:
EMAIL ADDRESS:	WITNESS SIGNATURE:
ADDRESS:	

DOCUMENT TYPE:	DATE/TIME NOTARIZED:	DOCUMENT DATE:	FEE CHARGED:

COMMENTS:	RECORD NUMBER: **86**

NOTARY LOG

FULL NAME:	PHONE NUMBER:	THUMB PRINT
EMAIL ADDRESS:	SIGNER'S SIGNATURE	
ADDRESS:		

SERVICE PERFORMED:	IDENTIFICATION	ID NUMBER:
❑ JURAT	❑ ID CARD ❑ CREDIBLE WITNESS	
❑ OATH	❑ PASSPORT ❑ KNOWN PERSONALLY	ISSUED BY:
❑ ACKNOWLEDGEMENT	❑ DRIVER'S LICENSE	
❑ OTHER: _____	❑ OTHER: _____	DATE ISSUED: / EXPIRATION DATE:

WITNESS FULL NAME:	PHONE NUMBER:
EMAIL ADDRESS:	WITNESS SIGNATURE:
ADDRESS:	

DOCUMENT TYPE:	DATE/TIME NOTARIZED:	DOCUMENT DATE:	FEE CHARGED:

COMMENTS:		RECORD NUMBER: 87

NOTARY LOG

FULL NAME:	PHONE NUMBER:	THUMB PRINT
EMAIL ADDRESS:	SIGNER'S SIGNATURE	
ADDRESS:		

SERVICE PERFORMED:	IDENTIFICATION	ID NUMBER:
❑ JURAT	❑ ID CARD ❑ CREDIBLE WITNESS	
❑ OATH	❑ PASSPORT ❑ KNOWN PERSONALLY	ISSUED BY:
❑ ACKNOWLEDGEMENT	❑ DRIVER'S LICENSE	
❑ OTHER: _____	❑ OTHER: _____	DATE ISSUED: / EXPIRATION DATE:

WITNESS FULL NAME:	PHONE NUMBER:
EMAIL ADDRESS:	WITNESS SIGNATURE:
ADDRESS:	

DOCUMENT TYPE:	DATE/TIME NOTARIZED:	DOCUMENT DATE:	FEE CHARGED:

COMMENTS:		RECORD NUMBER: 88

NOTARY LOG

FULL NAME:	PHONE NUMBER:	THUMB PRINT
EMAIL ADDRESS:	SIGNER'S SIGNATURE	
ADDRESS:		

SERVICE PERFORMED:	IDENTIFICATION	ID NUMBER:
❑ JURAT	❑ ID CARD ❑ CREDIBLE WITNESS	
❑ OATH	❑ PASSPORT ❑ KNOWN PERSONALLY	ISSUED BY:
❑ ACKNOWLEDGEMENT	❑ DRIVER'S LICENSE	
❑ OTHER: _____	❑ OTHER: _____	DATE ISSUED: / EXPIRATION DATE:

WITNESS FULL NAME:	PHONE NUMBER:
EMAIL ADDRESS:	WITNESS SIGNATURE:
ADDRESS:	

DOCUMENT TYPE:	DATE/TIME NOTARIZED:	DOCUMENT DATE:	FEE CHARGED:

COMMENTS:		RECORD NUMBER: **89**

NOTARY LOG

FULL NAME:	PHONE NUMBER:	THUMB PRINT
EMAIL ADDRESS:	SIGNER'S SIGNATURE	
ADDRESS:		

SERVICE PERFORMED:	IDENTIFICATION	ID NUMBER:
❑ JURAT	❑ ID CARD ❑ CREDIBLE WITNESS	
❑ OATH	❑ PASSPORT ❑ KNOWN PERSONALLY	ISSUED BY:
❑ ACKNOWLEDGEMENT	❑ DRIVER'S LICENSE	
❑ OTHER: _____	❑ OTHER: _____	DATE ISSUED: / EXPIRATION DATE:

WITNESS FULL NAME:	PHONE NUMBER:
EMAIL ADDRESS:	WITNESS SIGNATURE:
ADDRESS:	

DOCUMENT TYPE:	DATE/TIME NOTARIZED:	DOCUMENT DATE:	FEE CHARGED:

COMMENTS:		RECORD NUMBER: **90**

NOTARY LOG

FULL NAME:	PHONE NUMBER:	THUMB PRINT

EMAIL ADDRESS:

ADDRESS:

SIGNER'S SIGNATURE

SERVICE PERFORMED:	IDENTIFICATION	ID NUMBER:
❑ JURAT	❑ ID CARD ❑ CREDIBLE WITNESS	
❑ OATH	❑ PASSPORT ❑ KNOWN PERSONALLY	ISSUED BY:
❑ ACKNOWLEDGEMENT	❑ DRIVER'S LICENSE	
❑ OTHER: _____	❑ OTHER: _____	DATE ISSUED: / EXPIRATION DATE:

WITNESS FULL NAME: **PHONE NUMBER:**

EMAIL ADDRESS:

ADDRESS:

WITNESS SIGNATURE:

DOCUMENT TYPE:	DATE/TIME NOTARIZED:	DOCUMENT DATE:	FEE CHARGED:

COMMENTS:		RECORD NUMBER: **91**

NOTARY LOG

FULL NAME:	PHONE NUMBER:	THUMB PRINT

EMAIL ADDRESS:

ADDRESS:

SIGNER'S SIGNATURE

SERVICE PERFORMED:	IDENTIFICATION	ID NUMBER:
❑ JURAT	❑ ID CARD ❑ CREDIBLE WITNESS	
❑ OATH	❑ PASSPORT ❑ KNOWN PERSONALLY	ISSUED BY:
❑ ACKNOWLEDGEMENT	❑ DRIVER'S LICENSE	
❑ OTHER: _____	❑ OTHER: _____	DATE ISSUED: / EXPIRATION DATE:

WITNESS FULL NAME: **PHONE NUMBER:**

EMAIL ADDRESS:

ADDRESS:

WITNESS SIGNATURE:

DOCUMENT TYPE:	DATE/TIME NOTARIZED:	DOCUMENT DATE:	FEE CHARGED:

COMMENTS:		RECORD NUMBER: **92**

NOTARY LOG

FULL NAME:

PHONE NUMBER:

THUMB PRINT

EMAIL ADDRESS:

SIGNER'S SIGNATURE

ADDRESS:

SERVICE PERFORMED:
- ❑ JURAT
- ❑ OATH
- ❑ ACKNOWLEDGEMENT
- ❑ OTHER: _____

IDENTIFICATION
- ❑ ID CARD
- ❑ PASSPORT
- ❑ DRIVER'S LICENSE
- ❑ OTHER: _____
- ❑ CREDIBLE WITNESS
- ❑ KNOWN PERSONALLY

ID NUMBER:

ISSUED BY:

DATE ISSUED: | **EXPIRATION DATE:**

WITNESS FULL NAME:

PHONE NUMBER:

EMAIL ADDRESS:

WITNESS SIGNATURE:

ADDRESS:

DOCUMENT TYPE: | **DATE/TIME NOTARIZED:** | **DOCUMENT DATE:** | **FEE CHARGED:**

COMMENTS:

RECORD NUMBER: 93

NOTARY LOG

FULL NAME:

PHONE NUMBER:

THUMB PRINT

EMAIL ADDRESS:

SIGNER'S SIGNATURE

ADDRESS:

SERVICE PERFORMED:
- ❑ JURAT
- ❑ OATH
- ❑ ACKNOWLEDGEMENT
- ❑ OTHER: _____

IDENTIFICATION
- ❑ ID CARD
- ❑ PASSPORT
- ❑ DRIVER'S LICENSE
- ❑ OTHER: _____
- ❑ CREDIBLE WITNESS
- ❑ KNOWN PERSONALLY

ID NUMBER:

ISSUED BY:

DATE ISSUED: | **EXPIRATION DATE:**

WITNESS FULL NAME:

PHONE NUMBER:

EMAIL ADDRESS:

WITNESS SIGNATURE:

ADDRESS:

DOCUMENT TYPE: | **DATE/TIME NOTARIZED:** | **DOCUMENT DATE:** | **FEE CHARGED:**

COMMENTS:

RECORD NUMBER: 94

NOTARY LOG

FULL NAME:	PHONE NUMBER:	THUMB PRINT
EMAIL ADDRESS:	SIGNER'S SIGNATURE	
ADDRESS:		

SERVICE PERFORMED:	IDENTIFICATION	ID NUMBER:
❑ JURAT	❑ ID CARD ❑ CREDIBLE WITNESS	
❑ OATH	❑ PASSPORT ❑ KNOWN PERSONALLY	ISSUED BY:
❑ ACKNOWLEDGEMENT	❑ DRIVER'S LICENSE	
❑ OTHER: _____	❑ OTHER: _____	DATE ISSUED: EXPIRATION DATE:

WITNESS FULL NAME:	PHONE NUMBER:
EMAIL ADDRESS:	WITNESS SIGNATURE:
ADDRESS:	

DOCUMENT TYPE:	DATE/TIME NOTARIZED:	DOCUMENT DATE:	FEE CHARGED:
COMMENTS:			RECORD NUMBER: **95**

NOTARY LOG

FULL NAME:	PHONE NUMBER:	THUMB PRINT
EMAIL ADDRESS:	SIGNER'S SIGNATURE	
ADDRESS:		

SERVICE PERFORMED:	IDENTIFICATION	ID NUMBER:
❑ JURAT	❑ ID CARD ❑ CREDIBLE WITNESS	
❑ OATH	❑ PASSPORT ❑ KNOWN PERSONALLY	ISSUED BY:
❑ ACKNOWLEDGEMENT	❑ DRIVER'S LICENSE	
❑ OTHER: _____	❑ OTHER: _____	DATE ISSUED: EXPIRATION DATE:

WITNESS FULL NAME:	PHONE NUMBER:
EMAIL ADDRESS:	WITNESS SIGNATURE:
ADDRESS:	

DOCUMENT TYPE:	DATE/TIME NOTARIZED:	DOCUMENT DATE:	FEE CHARGED:
COMMENTS:			RECORD NUMBER: **96**

NOTARY LOG

FULL NAME:	PHONE NUMBER:	THUMB PRINT
EMAIL ADDRESS:	SIGNER'S SIGNATURE	
ADDRESS:		

SERVICE PERFORMED:
- ❑ JURAT
- ❑ OATH
- ❑ ACKNOWLEDGEMENT
- ❑ OTHER: _____

IDENTIFICATION
- ❑ ID CARD
- ❑ PASSPORT
- ❑ DRIVER'S LICENSE
- ❑ OTHER: _____
- ❑ CREDIBLE WITNESS
- ❑ KNOWN PERSONALLY

ID NUMBER:

ISSUED BY:

DATE ISSUED:	EXPIRATION DATE:

WITNESS FULL NAME:	PHONE NUMBER:
EMAIL ADDRESS:	WITNESS SIGNATURE:
ADDRESS:	

DOCUMENT TYPE:	DATE/TIME NOTARIZED:	DOCUMENT DATE:	FEE CHARGED:

COMMENTS:		RECORD NUMBER: **97**

NOTARY LOG

FULL NAME:	PHONE NUMBER:	THUMB PRINT
EMAIL ADDRESS:	SIGNER'S SIGNATURE	
ADDRESS:		

SERVICE PERFORMED:
- ❑ JURAT
- ❑ OATH
- ❑ ACKNOWLEDGEMENT
- ❑ OTHER: _____

IDENTIFICATION
- ❑ ID CARD
- ❑ PASSPORT
- ❑ DRIVER'S LICENSE
- ❑ OTHER: _____
- ❑ CREDIBLE WITNESS
- ❑ KNOWN PERSONALLY

ID NUMBER:

ISSUED BY:

DATE ISSUED:	EXPIRATION DATE:

WITNESS FULL NAME:	PHONE NUMBER:
EMAIL ADDRESS:	WITNESS SIGNATURE:
ADDRESS:	

DOCUMENT TYPE:	DATE/TIME NOTARIZED:	DOCUMENT DATE:	FEE CHARGED:

COMMENTS:		RECORD NUMBER: **98**

NOTARY LOG

FULL NAME:	PHONE NUMBER:	THUMB PRINT
EMAIL ADDRESS:	SIGNER'S SIGNATURE	
ADDRESS:		

SERVICE PERFORMED:	IDENTIFICATION	ID NUMBER:
❑ JURAT	❑ ID CARD ❑ CREDIBLE WITNESS	
❑ OATH	❑ PASSPORT ❑ KNOWN PERSONALLY	ISSUED BY:
❑ ACKNOWLEDGEMENT	❑ DRIVER'S LICENSE	DATE ISSUED: / EXPIRATION DATE:
❑ OTHER: _____	❑ OTHER: _____	

WITNESS FULL NAME:	PHONE NUMBER:
EMAIL ADDRESS:	WITNESS SIGNATURE:
ADDRESS:	

DOCUMENT TYPE:	DATE/TIME NOTARIZED:	DOCUMENT DATE:	FEE CHARGED:

COMMENTS:		RECORD NUMBER: **99**

NOTARY LOG

FULL NAME:	PHONE NUMBER:	THUMB PRINT
EMAIL ADDRESS:	SIGNER'S SIGNATURE	
ADDRESS:		

SERVICE PERFORMED:	IDENTIFICATION	ID NUMBER:
❑ JURAT	❑ ID CARD ❑ CREDIBLE WITNESS	
❑ OATH	❑ PASSPORT ❑ KNOWN PERSONALLY	ISSUED BY:
❑ ACKNOWLEDGEMENT	❑ DRIVER'S LICENSE	DATE ISSUED: / EXPIRATION DATE:
❑ OTHER: _____	❑ OTHER: _____	

WITNESS FULL NAME:	PHONE NUMBER:
EMAIL ADDRESS:	WITNESS SIGNATURE:
ADDRESS:	

DOCUMENT TYPE:	DATE/TIME NOTARIZED:	DOCUMENT DATE:	FEE CHARGED:

COMMENTS:		RECORD NUMBER: **100**

NOTARY LOG

FULL NAME:		PHONE NUMBER:	THUMB PRINT
EMAIL ADDRESS:		SIGNER'S SIGNATURE	
ADDRESS:			

SERVICE PERFORMED:	IDENTIFICATION		ID NUMBER:
❑ JURAT	❑ ID CARD	❑ CREDIBLE WITNESS	
❑ OATH	❑ PASSPORT	❑ KNOWN PERSONALLY	ISSUED BY:
❑ ACKNOWLEDGEMENT	❑ DRIVER'S LICENSE		
❑ OTHER: _____	❑ OTHER: _____		DATE ISSUED: EXPIRATION DATE:

WITNESS FULL NAME:	PHONE NUMBER:
EMAIL ADDRESS:	WITNESS SIGNATURE:
ADDRESS:	

DOCUMENT TYPE:	DATE/TIME NOTARIZED:	DOCUMENT DATE:	FEE CHARGED:
COMMENTS:			RECORD NUMBER: **101**

NOTARY LOG

FULL NAME:		PHONE NUMBER:	THUMB PRINT
EMAIL ADDRESS:		SIGNER'S SIGNATURE	
ADDRESS:			

SERVICE PERFORMED:	IDENTIFICATION		ID NUMBER:
❑ JURAT	❑ ID CARD	❑ CREDIBLE WITNESS	
❑ OATH	❑ PASSPORT	❑ KNOWN PERSONALLY	ISSUED BY:
❑ ACKNOWLEDGEMENT	❑ DRIVER'S LICENSE		
❑ OTHER: _____	❑ OTHER: _____		DATE ISSUED: EXPIRATION DATE:

WITNESS FULL NAME:	PHONE NUMBER:
EMAIL ADDRESS:	WITNESS SIGNATURE:
ADDRESS:	

DOCUMENT TYPE:	DATE/TIME NOTARIZED:	DOCUMENT DATE:	FEE CHARGED:
COMMENTS:			RECORD NUMBER: **102**

NOTARY LOG

FULL NAME:	PHONE NUMBER:	THUMB PRINT
EMAIL ADDRESS:	SIGNER'S SIGNATURE	
ADDRESS:		

SERVICE PERFORMED:	IDENTIFICATION	ID NUMBER:
❏ JURAT	❏ ID CARD ❏ CREDIBLE WITNESS	
❏ OATH	❏ PASSPORT ❏ KNOWN PERSONALLY	ISSUED BY:
❏ ACKNOWLEDGEMENT	❏ DRIVER'S LICENSE	
❏ OTHER: _____	❏ OTHER: _____	DATE ISSUED: EXPIRATION DATE:

WITNESS FULL NAME:	PHONE NUMBER:
EMAIL ADDRESS:	WITNESS SIGNATURE:
ADDRESS:	

DOCUMENT TYPE:	DATE/TIME NOTARIZED:	DOCUMENT DATE:	FEE CHARGED:

COMMENTS:		RECORD NUMBER: **103**

NOTARY LOG

FULL NAME:	PHONE NUMBER:	THUMB PRINT
EMAIL ADDRESS:	SIGNER'S SIGNATURE	
ADDRESS:		

SERVICE PERFORMED:	IDENTIFICATION	ID NUMBER:
❏ JURAT	❏ ID CARD ❏ CREDIBLE WITNESS	
❏ OATH	❏ PASSPORT ❏ KNOWN PERSONALLY	ISSUED BY:
❏ ACKNOWLEDGEMENT	❏ DRIVER'S LICENSE	
❏ OTHER: _____	❏ OTHER: _____	DATE ISSUED: EXPIRATION DATE:

WITNESS FULL NAME:	PHONE NUMBER:
EMAIL ADDRESS:	WITNESS SIGNATURE:
ADDRESS:	

DOCUMENT TYPE:	DATE/TIME NOTARIZED:	DOCUMENT DATE:	FEE CHARGED:

COMMENTS:		RECORD NUMBER: **104**

NOTARY LOG

FULL NAME:	**PHONE NUMBER:**	**THUMB PRINT**
EMAIL ADDRESS:	**SIGNER'S SIGNATURE**	
ADDRESS:		

SERVICE PERFORMED:
- ❑ JURAT
- ❑ OATH
- ❑ ACKNOWLEDGEMENT
- ❑ OTHER: _____

IDENTIFICATION
- ❑ ID CARD
- ❑ PASSPORT
- ❑ DRIVER'S LICENSE
- ❑ OTHER: _____
- ❑ CREDIBLE WITNESS
- ❑ KNOWN PERSONALLY

ID NUMBER:

ISSUED BY:

DATE ISSUED: **EXPIRATION DATE:**

WITNESS FULL NAME:	**PHONE NUMBER:**
EMAIL ADDRESS:	**WITNESS SIGNATURE:**
ADDRESS:	

DOCUMENT TYPE:	**DATE/TIME NOTARIZED:**	**DOCUMENT DATE:**	**FEE CHARGED:**

COMMENTS:

RECORD NUMBER: 105

NOTARY LOG

FULL NAME:	**PHONE NUMBER:**	**THUMB PRINT**
EMAIL ADDRESS:	**SIGNER'S SIGNATURE**	
ADDRESS:		

SERVICE PERFORMED:
- ❑ JURAT
- ❑ OATH
- ❑ ACKNOWLEDGEMENT
- ❑ OTHER: _____

IDENTIFICATION
- ❑ ID CARD
- ❑ PASSPORT
- ❑ DRIVER'S LICENSE
- ❑ OTHER: _____
- ❑ CREDIBLE WITNESS
- ❑ KNOWN PERSONALLY

ID NUMBER:

ISSUED BY:

DATE ISSUED: **EXPIRATION DATE:**

WITNESS FULL NAME:	**PHONE NUMBER:**
EMAIL ADDRESS:	**WITNESS SIGNATURE:**
ADDRESS:	

DOCUMENT TYPE:	**DATE/TIME NOTARIZED:**	**DOCUMENT DATE:**	**FEE CHARGED:**

COMMENTS:

RECORD NUMBER: 106

NOTARY LOG

FULL NAME:	PHONE NUMBER:	THUMB PRINT
EMAIL ADDRESS:	SIGNER'S SIGNATURE	
ADDRESS:		

SERVICE PERFORMED:
- ❏ JURAT
- ❏ OATH
- ❏ ACKNOWLEDGEMENT
- ❏ OTHER: _____

IDENTIFICATION
- ❏ ID CARD
- ❏ PASSPORT
- ❏ DRIVER'S LICENSE
- ❏ OTHER: _____
- ❏ CREDIBLE WITNESS
- ❏ KNOWN PERSONALLY

ID NUMBER:

ISSUED BY:

DATE ISSUED: | EXPIRATION DATE:

WITNESS FULL NAME:	PHONE NUMBER:
EMAIL ADDRESS:	WITNESS SIGNATURE:
ADDRESS:	

DOCUMENT TYPE:	DATE/TIME NOTARIZED:	DOCUMENT DATE:	FEE CHARGED:
COMMENTS:			RECORD NUMBER: **107**

NOTARY LOG

FULL NAME:	PHONE NUMBER:	THUMB PRINT
EMAIL ADDRESS:	SIGNER'S SIGNATURE	
ADDRESS:		

SERVICE PERFORMED:
- ❏ JURAT
- ❏ OATH
- ❏ ACKNOWLEDGEMENT
- ❏ OTHER: _____

IDENTIFICATION
- ❏ ID CARD
- ❏ PASSPORT
- ❏ DRIVER'S LICENSE
- ❏ OTHER: _____
- ❏ CREDIBLE WITNESS
- ❏ KNOWN PERSONALLY

ID NUMBER:

ISSUED BY:

DATE ISSUED: | EXPIRATION DATE:

WITNESS FULL NAME:	PHONE NUMBER:
EMAIL ADDRESS:	WITNESS SIGNATURE:
ADDRESS:	

DOCUMENT TYPE:	DATE/TIME NOTARIZED:	DOCUMENT DATE:	FEE CHARGED:
COMMENTS:			RECORD NUMBER: **108**

NOTARY LOG

FULL NAME:		PHONE NUMBER:	THUMB PRINT
EMAIL ADDRESS:		SIGNER'S SIGNATURE	
ADDRESS:			

SERVICE PERFORMED:	IDENTIFICATION	ID NUMBER:
❑ JURAT	❑ ID CARD ❑ CREDIBLE WITNESS	
❑ OATH	❑ PASSPORT ❑ KNOWN PERSONALLY	ISSUED BY:
❑ ACKNOWLEDGEMENT	❑ DRIVER'S LICENSE	
❑ OTHER: _____	❑ OTHER: _____	DATE ISSUED: EXPIRATION DATE:

WITNESS FULL NAME:	PHONE NUMBER:
EMAIL ADDRESS:	WITNESS SIGNATURE:
ADDRESS:	

DOCUMENT TYPE:	DATE/TIME NOTARIZED:	DOCUMENT DATE:	FEE CHARGED:
COMMENTS:			RECORD NUMBER: **109**

NOTARY LOG

FULL NAME:		PHONE NUMBER:	THUMB PRINT
EMAIL ADDRESS:		SIGNER'S SIGNATURE	
ADDRESS:			

SERVICE PERFORMED:	IDENTIFICATION	ID NUMBER:
❑ JURAT	❑ ID CARD ❑ CREDIBLE WITNESS	
❑ OATH	❑ PASSPORT ❑ KNOWN PERSONALLY	ISSUED BY:
❑ ACKNOWLEDGEMENT	❑ DRIVER'S LICENSE	
❑ OTHER: _____	❑ OTHER: _____	DATE ISSUED: EXPIRATION DATE:

WITNESS FULL NAME:	PHONE NUMBER:
EMAIL ADDRESS:	WITNESS SIGNATURE:
ADDRESS:	

DOCUMENT TYPE:	DATE/TIME NOTARIZED:	DOCUMENT DATE:	FEE CHARGED:
COMMENTS:			RECORD NUMBER: **110**

NOTARY LOG

FULL NAME:	PHONE NUMBER:	THUMB PRINT
EMAIL ADDRESS:	SIGNER'S SIGNATURE	
ADDRESS:		

SERVICE PERFORMED:
- ❑ JURAT
- ❑ OATH
- ❑ ACKNOWLEDGEMENT
- ❑ OTHER: _____

IDENTIFICATION
- ❑ ID CARD
- ❑ PASSPORT
- ❑ DRIVER'S LICENSE
- ❑ OTHER: _____
- ❑ CREDIBLE WITNESS
- ❑ KNOWN PERSONALLY

ID NUMBER:

ISSUED BY:

DATE ISSUED: EXPIRATION DATE:

WITNESS FULL NAME:	PHONE NUMBER:
EMAIL ADDRESS:	WITNESS SIGNATURE:
ADDRESS:	

DOCUMENT TYPE:	DATE/TIME NOTARIZED:	DOCUMENT DATE:	FEE CHARGED:

COMMENTS:		RECORD NUMBER: **111**

NOTARY LOG

FULL NAME:	PHONE NUMBER:	THUMB PRINT
EMAIL ADDRESS:	SIGNER'S SIGNATURE	
ADDRESS:		

SERVICE PERFORMED:
- ❑ JURAT
- ❑ OATH
- ❑ ACKNOWLEDGEMENT
- ❑ OTHER: _____

IDENTIFICATION
- ❑ ID CARD
- ❑ PASSPORT
- ❑ DRIVER'S LICENSE
- ❑ OTHER: _____
- ❑ CREDIBLE WITNESS
- ❑ KNOWN PERSONALLY

ID NUMBER:

ISSUED BY:

DATE ISSUED: EXPIRATION DATE:

WITNESS FULL NAME:	PHONE NUMBER:
EMAIL ADDRESS:	WITNESS SIGNATURE:
ADDRESS:	

DOCUMENT TYPE:	DATE/TIME NOTARIZED:	DOCUMENT DATE:	FEE CHARGED:

COMMENTS:		RECORD NUMBER: **112**

NOTARY LOG

FULL NAME:

PHONE NUMBER:

THUMB PRINT

EMAIL ADDRESS:

SIGNER'S SIGNATURE

ADDRESS:

SERVICE PERFORMED:
- ❑ JURAT
- ❑ OATH
- ❑ ACKNOWLEDGEMENT
- ❑ OTHER: _____

IDENTIFICATION
- ❑ ID CARD
- ❑ PASSPORT
- ❑ DRIVER'S LICENSE
- ❑ OTHER: _____
- ❑ CREDIBLE WITNESS
- ❑ KNOWN PERSONALLY

ID NUMBER:

ISSUED BY:

DATE ISSUED:

EXPIRATION DATE:

WITNESS FULL NAME:

PHONE NUMBER:

EMAIL ADDRESS:

WITNESS SIGNATURE:

ADDRESS:

DOCUMENT TYPE:

DATE/TIME NOTARIZED:

DOCUMENT DATE:

FEE CHARGED:

COMMENTS:

RECORD NUMBER: **113**

NOTARY LOG

FULL NAME:

PHONE NUMBER:

THUMB PRINT

EMAIL ADDRESS:

SIGNER'S SIGNATURE

ADDRESS:

SERVICE PERFORMED:
- ❑ JURAT
- ❑ OATH
- ❑ ACKNOWLEDGEMENT
- ❑ OTHER: _____

IDENTIFICATION
- ❑ ID CARD
- ❑ PASSPORT
- ❑ DRIVER'S LICENSE
- ❑ OTHER: _____
- ❑ CREDIBLE WITNESS
- ❑ KNOWN PERSONALLY

ID NUMBER:

ISSUED BY:

DATE ISSUED:

EXPIRATION DATE:

WITNESS FULL NAME:

PHONE NUMBER:

EMAIL ADDRESS:

WITNESS SIGNATURE:

ADDRESS:

DOCUMENT TYPE:

DATE/TIME NOTARIZED:

DOCUMENT DATE:

FEE CHARGED:

COMMENTS:

RECORD NUMBER: **114**

NOTARY LOG

FULL NAME:	PHONE NUMBER:	THUMB PRINT
EMAIL ADDRESS:	SIGNER'S SIGNATURE	
ADDRESS:		

SERVICE PERFORMED:
- ❏ JURAT
- ❏ OATH
- ❏ ACKNOWLEDGEMENT
- ❏ OTHER: _____

IDENTIFICATION
- ❏ ID CARD
- ❏ PASSPORT
- ❏ DRIVER'S LICENSE
- ❏ OTHER: _____
- ❏ CREDIBLE WITNESS
- ❏ KNOWN PERSONALLY

ID NUMBER:

ISSUED BY:

DATE ISSUED:

EXPIRATION DATE:

WITNESS FULL NAME:

PHONE NUMBER:

EMAIL ADDRESS:

WITNESS SIGNATURE:

ADDRESS:

DOCUMENT TYPE:	DATE/TIME NOTARIZED:	DOCUMENT DATE:	FEE CHARGED:

COMMENTS:

RECORD NUMBER: **115**

NOTARY LOG

FULL NAME:	PHONE NUMBER:	THUMB PRINT
EMAIL ADDRESS:	SIGNER'S SIGNATURE	
ADDRESS:		

SERVICE PERFORMED:
- ❏ JURAT
- ❏ OATH
- ❏ ACKNOWLEDGEMENT
- ❏ OTHER: _____

IDENTIFICATION
- ❏ ID CARD
- ❏ PASSPORT
- ❏ DRIVER'S LICENSE
- ❏ OTHER: _____
- ❏ CREDIBLE WITNESS
- ❏ KNOWN PERSONALLY

ID NUMBER:

ISSUED BY:

DATE ISSUED:

EXPIRATION DATE:

WITNESS FULL NAME:

PHONE NUMBER:

EMAIL ADDRESS:

WITNESS SIGNATURE:

ADDRESS:

DOCUMENT TYPE:	DATE/TIME NOTARIZED:	DOCUMENT DATE:	FEE CHARGED:

COMMENTS:

RECORD NUMBER: **116**

NOTARY LOG

FULL NAME:

PHONE NUMBER:

THUMB PRINT

EMAIL ADDRESS:

SIGNER'S SIGNATURE

ADDRESS:

SERVICE PERFORMED:
- ❑ JURAT
- ❑ OATH
- ❑ ACKNOWLEDGEMENT
- ❑ OTHER: _____

IDENTIFICATION
- ❑ ID CARD
- ❑ PASSPORT
- ❑ DRIVER'S LICENSE
- ❑ OTHER: _____
- ❑ CREDIBLE WITNESS
- ❑ KNOWN PERSONALLY

ID NUMBER:

ISSUED BY:

DATE ISSUED:

EXPIRATION DATE:

WITNESS FULL NAME:

PHONE NUMBER:

EMAIL ADDRESS:

WITNESS SIGNATURE:

ADDRESS:

DOCUMENT TYPE:

DATE/TIME NOTARIZED:

DOCUMENT DATE:

FEE CHARGED:

COMMENTS:

RECORD NUMBER: 117

NOTARY LOG

FULL NAME:

PHONE NUMBER:

THUMB PRINT

EMAIL ADDRESS:

SIGNER'S SIGNATURE

ADDRESS:

SERVICE PERFORMED:
- ❑ JURAT
- ❑ OATH
- ❑ ACKNOWLEDGEMENT
- ❑ OTHER: _____

IDENTIFICATION
- ❑ ID CARD
- ❑ PASSPORT
- ❑ DRIVER'S LICENSE
- ❑ OTHER: _____
- ❑ CREDIBLE WITNESS
- ❑ KNOWN PERSONALLY

ID NUMBER:

ISSUED BY:

DATE ISSUED:

EXPIRATION DATE:

WITNESS FULL NAME:

PHONE NUMBER:

EMAIL ADDRESS:

WITNESS SIGNATURE:

ADDRESS:

DOCUMENT TYPE:

DATE/TIME NOTARIZED:

DOCUMENT DATE:

FEE CHARGED:

COMMENTS:

RECORD NUMBER: 118

NOTARY LOG

FULL NAME:	PHONE NUMBER:	THUMB PRINT
EMAIL ADDRESS:	SIGNER'S SIGNATURE	
ADDRESS:		

SERVICE PERFORMED:	IDENTIFICATION	ID NUMBER:
❑ JURAT	❑ ID CARD ❑ CREDIBLE WITNESS	
❑ OATH	❑ PASSPORT ❑ KNOWN PERSONALLY	ISSUED BY:
❑ ACKNOWLEDGEMENT	❑ DRIVER'S LICENSE	
❑ OTHER: _____	❑ OTHER: _____	DATE ISSUED: EXPIRATION DATE:

WITNESS FULL NAME:	PHONE NUMBER:
EMAIL ADDRESS:	WITNESS SIGNATURE:
ADDRESS:	

DOCUMENT TYPE:	DATE/TIME NOTARIZED:	DOCUMENT DATE:	FEE CHARGED:

COMMENTS:		RECORD NUMBER: **119**

NOTARY LOG

FULL NAME:	PHONE NUMBER:	THUMB PRINT
EMAIL ADDRESS:	SIGNER'S SIGNATURE	
ADDRESS:		

SERVICE PERFORMED:	IDENTIFICATION	ID NUMBER:
❑ JURAT	❑ ID CARD ❑ CREDIBLE WITNESS	
❑ OATH	❑ PASSPORT ❑ KNOWN PERSONALLY	ISSUED BY:
❑ ACKNOWLEDGEMENT	❑ DRIVER'S LICENSE	
❑ OTHER: _____	❑ OTHER: _____	DATE ISSUED: EXPIRATION DATE:

WITNESS FULL NAME:	PHONE NUMBER:
EMAIL ADDRESS:	WITNESS SIGNATURE:
ADDRESS:	

DOCUMENT TYPE:	DATE/TIME NOTARIZED:	DOCUMENT DATE:	FEE CHARGED:

COMMENTS:		RECORD NUMBER: **120**

NOTARY LOG

FULL NAME:	PHONE NUMBER:	THUMB PRINT
EMAIL ADDRESS:	SIGNER'S SIGNATURE	
ADDRESS:		

SERVICE PERFORMED:	IDENTIFICATION	ID NUMBER:
❏ JURAT	❏ ID CARD ❏ CREDIBLE WITNESS	
❏ OATH	❏ PASSPORT ❏ KNOWN PERSONALLY	ISSUED BY:
❏ ACKNOWLEDGEMENT	❏ DRIVER'S LICENSE	
❏ OTHER: _____	❏ OTHER: _____	DATE ISSUED: EXPIRATION DATE:

WITNESS FULL NAME:	PHONE NUMBER:
EMAIL ADDRESS:	WITNESS SIGNATURE:
ADDRESS:	

DOCUMENT TYPE:	DATE/TIME NOTARIZED:	DOCUMENT DATE:	FEE CHARGED:

COMMENTS:		RECORD NUMBER: 121

NOTARY LOG

FULL NAME:	PHONE NUMBER:	THUMB PRINT
EMAIL ADDRESS:	SIGNER'S SIGNATURE	
ADDRESS:		

SERVICE PERFORMED:	IDENTIFICATION	ID NUMBER:
❏ JURAT	❏ ID CARD ❏ CREDIBLE WITNESS	
❏ OATH	❏ PASSPORT ❏ KNOWN PERSONALLY	ISSUED BY:
❏ ACKNOWLEDGEMENT	❏ DRIVER'S LICENSE	
❏ OTHER: _____	❏ OTHER: _____	DATE ISSUED: EXPIRATION DATE:

WITNESS FULL NAME:	PHONE NUMBER:
EMAIL ADDRESS:	WITNESS SIGNATURE:
ADDRESS:	

DOCUMENT TYPE:	DATE/TIME NOTARIZED:	DOCUMENT DATE:	FEE CHARGED:

COMMENTS:		RECORD NUMBER: 122

NOTARY LOG

FULL NAME:	PHONE NUMBER:	THUMB PRINT
EMAIL ADDRESS:	SIGNER'S SIGNATURE	
ADDRESS:		

SERVICE PERFORMED:
- ❑ JURAT
- ❑ OATH
- ❑ ACKNOWLEDGEMENT
- ❑ OTHER: _____

IDENTIFICATION
- ❑ ID CARD
- ❑ PASSPORT
- ❑ DRIVER'S LICENSE
- ❑ OTHER: _____
- ❑ CREDIBLE WITNESS
- ❑ KNOWN PERSONALLY

ID NUMBER:

ISSUED BY:

DATE ISSUED: | EXPIRATION DATE:

WITNESS FULL NAME: | PHONE NUMBER:

EMAIL ADDRESS: | WITNESS SIGNATURE:

ADDRESS:

DOCUMENT TYPE:	DATE/TIME NOTARIZED:	DOCUMENT DATE:	FEE CHARGED:

COMMENTS: | RECORD NUMBER: **123**

NOTARY LOG

FULL NAME:	PHONE NUMBER:	THUMB PRINT
EMAIL ADDRESS:	SIGNER'S SIGNATURE	
ADDRESS:		

SERVICE PERFORMED:
- ❑ JURAT
- ❑ OATH
- ❑ ACKNOWLEDGEMENT
- ❑ OTHER: _____

IDENTIFICATION
- ❑ ID CARD
- ❑ PASSPORT
- ❑ DRIVER'S LICENSE
- ❑ OTHER: _____
- ❑ CREDIBLE WITNESS
- ❑ KNOWN PERSONALLY

ID NUMBER:

ISSUED BY:

DATE ISSUED: | EXPIRATION DATE:

WITNESS FULL NAME: | PHONE NUMBER:

EMAIL ADDRESS: | WITNESS SIGNATURE:

ADDRESS:

DOCUMENT TYPE:	DATE/TIME NOTARIZED:	DOCUMENT DATE:	FEE CHARGED:

COMMENTS: | RECORD NUMBER: **124**

NOTARY LOG

FULL NAME:	PHONE NUMBER:	THUMB PRINT
EMAIL ADDRESS:	SIGNER'S SIGNATURE	
ADDRESS:		

SERVICE PERFORMED:	IDENTIFICATION		ID NUMBER:
❑ JURAT	❑ ID CARD	❑ CREDIBLE WITNESS	
❑ OATH	❑ PASSPORT	❑ KNOWN PERSONALLY	ISSUED BY:
❑ ACKNOWLEDGEMENT	❑ DRIVER'S LICENSE		
❑ OTHER: _____	❑ OTHER: _____		DATE ISSUED: / EXPIRATION DATE:

WITNESS FULL NAME:	PHONE NUMBER:
EMAIL ADDRESS:	WITNESS SIGNATURE:
ADDRESS:	

DOCUMENT TYPE:	DATE/TIME NOTARIZED:	DOCUMENT DATE:	FEE CHARGED:

COMMENTS:		RECORD NUMBER: 125

NOTARY LOG

FULL NAME:	PHONE NUMBER:	THUMB PRINT
EMAIL ADDRESS:	SIGNER'S SIGNATURE	
ADDRESS:		

SERVICE PERFORMED:	IDENTIFICATION		ID NUMBER:
❑ JURAT	❑ ID CARD	❑ CREDIBLE WITNESS	
❑ OATH	❑ PASSPORT	❑ KNOWN PERSONALLY	ISSUED BY:
❑ ACKNOWLEDGEMENT	❑ DRIVER'S LICENSE		
❑ OTHER: _____	❑ OTHER: _____		DATE ISSUED: / EXPIRATION DATE:

WITNESS FULL NAME:	PHONE NUMBER:
EMAIL ADDRESS:	WITNESS SIGNATURE:
ADDRESS:	

DOCUMENT TYPE:	DATE/TIME NOTARIZED:	DOCUMENT DATE:	FEE CHARGED:

COMMENTS:		RECORD NUMBER: 126

NOTARY LOG

FULL NAME:		PHONE NUMBER:	THUMB PRINT
EMAIL ADDRESS:		SIGNER'S SIGNATURE	
ADDRESS:			

SERVICE PERFORMED:	IDENTIFICATION	ID NUMBER:
☐ JURAT	☐ ID CARD ☐ CREDIBLE WITNESS	
☐ OATH	☐ PASSPORT ☐ KNOWN PERSONALLY	ISSUED BY:
☐ ACKNOWLEDGEMENT	☐ DRIVER'S LICENSE	
☐ OTHER: _____	☐ OTHER: _____	DATE ISSUED: EXPIRATION DATE:

WITNESS FULL NAME:		PHONE NUMBER:
EMAIL ADDRESS:		WITNESS SIGNATURE:
ADDRESS:		

DOCUMENT TYPE:	DATE/TIME NOTARIZED:	DOCUMENT DATE:	FEE CHARGED:
COMMENTS:			RECORD NUMBER: 127

NOTARY LOG

FULL NAME:		PHONE NUMBER:	THUMB PRINT
EMAIL ADDRESS:		SIGNER'S SIGNATURE	
ADDRESS:			

SERVICE PERFORMED:	IDENTIFICATION	ID NUMBER:
☐ JURAT	☐ ID CARD ☐ CREDIBLE WITNESS	
☐ OATH	☐ PASSPORT ☐ KNOWN PERSONALLY	ISSUED BY:
☐ ACKNOWLEDGEMENT	☐ DRIVER'S LICENSE	
☐ OTHER: _____	☐ OTHER: _____	DATE ISSUED: EXPIRATION DATE:

WITNESS FULL NAME:		PHONE NUMBER:
EMAIL ADDRESS:		WITNESS SIGNATURE:
ADDRESS:		

DOCUMENT TYPE:	DATE/TIME NOTARIZED:	DOCUMENT DATE:	FEE CHARGED:
COMMENTS:			RECORD NUMBER: 128

NOTARY LOG

FULL NAME:	PHONE NUMBER:	THUMB PRINT
EMAIL ADDRESS:	SIGNER'S SIGNATURE	
ADDRESS:		

SERVICE PERFORMED:	IDENTIFICATION	ID NUMBER:
❑ JURAT	❑ ID CARD ❑ CREDIBLE WITNESS	
❑ OATH	❑ PASSPORT ❑ KNOWN PERSONALLY	ISSUED BY:
❑ ACKNOWLEDGEMENT	❑ DRIVER'S LICENSE	
❑ OTHER: _____	❑ OTHER: _____	DATE ISSUED: EXPIRATION DATE:

WITNESS FULL NAME:	PHONE NUMBER:
EMAIL ADDRESS:	WITNESS SIGNATURE:
ADDRESS:	

DOCUMENT TYPE:	DATE/TIME NOTARIZED:	DOCUMENT DATE:	FEE CHARGED:

COMMENTS:		RECORD NUMBER: 129

NOTARY LOG

FULL NAME:	PHONE NUMBER:	THUMB PRINT
EMAIL ADDRESS:	SIGNER'S SIGNATURE	
ADDRESS:		

SERVICE PERFORMED:	IDENTIFICATION	ID NUMBER:
❑ JURAT	❑ ID CARD ❑ CREDIBLE WITNESS	
❑ OATH	❑ PASSPORT ❑ KNOWN PERSONALLY	ISSUED BY:
❑ ACKNOWLEDGEMENT	❑ DRIVER'S LICENSE	
❑ OTHER: _____	❑ OTHER: _____	DATE ISSUED: EXPIRATION DATE:

WITNESS FULL NAME:	PHONE NUMBER:
EMAIL ADDRESS:	WITNESS SIGNATURE:
ADDRESS:	

DOCUMENT TYPE:	DATE/TIME NOTARIZED:	DOCUMENT DATE:	FEE CHARGED:

COMMENTS:		RECORD NUMBER: 130

NOTARY LOG

FULL NAME:	PHONE NUMBER:	THUMB PRINT
EMAIL ADDRESS:	SIGNER'S SIGNATURE	
ADDRESS:		

SERVICE PERFORMED:
- ❑ JURAT
- ❑ OATH
- ❑ ACKNOWLEDGEMENT
- ❑ OTHER: _____

IDENTIFICATION
- ❑ ID CARD
- ❑ PASSPORT
- ❑ DRIVER'S LICENSE
- ❑ OTHER: _____
- ❑ CREDIBLE WITNESS
- ❑ KNOWN PERSONALLY

ID NUMBER:

ISSUED BY:

DATE ISSUED: EXPIRATION DATE:

WITNESS FULL NAME:	PHONE NUMBER:
EMAIL ADDRESS:	WITNESS SIGNATURE:
ADDRESS:	

DOCUMENT TYPE:	DATE/TIME NOTARIZED:	DOCUMENT DATE:	FEE CHARGED:

COMMENTS: RECORD NUMBER: **131**

NOTARY LOG

FULL NAME:	PHONE NUMBER:	THUMB PRINT
EMAIL ADDRESS:	SIGNER'S SIGNATURE	
ADDRESS:		

SERVICE PERFORMED:
- ❑ JURAT
- ❑ OATH
- ❑ ACKNOWLEDGEMENT
- ❑ OTHER: _____

IDENTIFICATION
- ❑ ID CARD
- ❑ PASSPORT
- ❑ DRIVER'S LICENSE
- ❑ OTHER: _____
- ❑ CREDIBLE WITNESS
- ❑ KNOWN PERSONALLY

ID NUMBER:

ISSUED BY:

DATE ISSUED: EXPIRATION DATE:

WITNESS FULL NAME:	PHONE NUMBER:
EMAIL ADDRESS:	WITNESS SIGNATURE:
ADDRESS:	

DOCUMENT TYPE:	DATE/TIME NOTARIZED:	DOCUMENT DATE:	FEE CHARGED:

COMMENTS: RECORD NUMBER: **132**

NOTARY LOG

FULL NAME:

PHONE NUMBER:

THUMB PRINT

EMAIL ADDRESS:

SIGNER'S SIGNATURE

ADDRESS:

SERVICE PERFORMED:

- ❑ JURAT
- ❑ OATH
- ❑ ACKNOWLEDGEMENT
- ❑ OTHER: _____

IDENTIFICATION

- ❑ ID CARD
- ❑ PASSPORT
- ❑ DRIVER'S LICENSE
- ❑ OTHER: _____

- ❑ CREDIBLE WITNESS
- ❑ KNOWN PERSONALLY

ID NUMBER:

ISSUED BY:

DATE ISSUED:

EXPIRATION DATE:

WITNESS FULL NAME:

PHONE NUMBER:

EMAIL ADDRESS:

WITNESS SIGNATURE:

ADDRESS:

DOCUMENT TYPE:

DATE/TIME NOTARIZED:

DOCUMENT DATE:

FEE CHARGED:

COMMENTS:

RECORD NUMBER: 133

NOTARY LOG

FULL NAME:

PHONE NUMBER:

THUMB PRINT

EMAIL ADDRESS:

SIGNER'S SIGNATURE

ADDRESS:

SERVICE PERFORMED:

- ❑ JURAT
- ❑ OATH
- ❑ ACKNOWLEDGEMENT
- ❑ OTHER: _____

IDENTIFICATION

- ❑ ID CARD
- ❑ PASSPORT
- ❑ DRIVER'S LICENSE
- ❑ OTHER: _____

- ❑ CREDIBLE WITNESS
- ❑ KNOWN PERSONALLY

ID NUMBER:

ISSUED BY:

DATE ISSUED:

EXPIRATION DATE:

WITNESS FULL NAME:

PHONE NUMBER:

EMAIL ADDRESS:

WITNESS SIGNATURE:

ADDRESS:

DOCUMENT TYPE:

DATE/TIME NOTARIZED:

DOCUMENT DATE:

FEE CHARGED:

COMMENTS:

RECORD NUMBER: 134

NOTARY LOG

FULL NAME:	PHONE NUMBER:	THUMB PRINT
EMAIL ADDRESS:	SIGNER'S SIGNATURE	
ADDRESS:		

SERVICE PERFORMED:
- ❏ JURAT
- ❏ OATH
- ❏ ACKNOWLEDGEMENT
- ❏ OTHER: _____

IDENTIFICATION
- ❏ ID CARD
- ❏ PASSPORT
- ❏ DRIVER'S LICENSE
- ❏ OTHER: _____
- ❏ CREDIBLE WITNESS
- ❏ KNOWN PERSONALLY

ID NUMBER:

ISSUED BY:

DATE ISSUED: EXPIRATION DATE:

WITNESS FULL NAME:	PHONE NUMBER:
EMAIL ADDRESS:	WITNESS SIGNATURE:
ADDRESS:	

DOCUMENT TYPE:	DATE/TIME NOTARIZED:	DOCUMENT DATE:	FEE CHARGED:
COMMENTS:			RECORD NUMBER: **135**

NOTARY LOG

FULL NAME:	PHONE NUMBER:	THUMB PRINT
EMAIL ADDRESS:	SIGNER'S SIGNATURE	
ADDRESS:		

SERVICE PERFORMED:
- ❏ JURAT
- ❏ OATH
- ❏ ACKNOWLEDGEMENT
- ❏ OTHER: _____

IDENTIFICATION
- ❏ ID CARD
- ❏ PASSPORT
- ❏ DRIVER'S LICENSE
- ❏ OTHER: _____
- ❏ CREDIBLE WITNESS
- ❏ KNOWN PERSONALLY

ID NUMBER:

ISSUED BY:

DATE ISSUED: EXPIRATION DATE:

WITNESS FULL NAME:	PHONE NUMBER:
EMAIL ADDRESS:	WITNESS SIGNATURE:
ADDRESS:	

DOCUMENT TYPE:	DATE/TIME NOTARIZED:	DOCUMENT DATE:	FEE CHARGED:
COMMENTS:			RECORD NUMBER: **136**

NOTARY LOG

FULL NAME:

PHONE NUMBER:

THUMB PRINT

EMAIL ADDRESS:

SIGNER'S SIGNATURE

ADDRESS:

SERVICE PERFORMED:
- ❏ JURAT
- ❏ OATH
- ❏ ACKNOWLEDGEMENT
- ❏ OTHER: _____

IDENTIFICATION
- ❏ ID CARD
- ❏ PASSPORT
- ❏ DRIVER'S LICENSE
- ❏ OTHER: _____
- ❏ CREDIBLE WITNESS
- ❏ KNOWN PERSONALLY

ID NUMBER:

ISSUED BY:

DATE ISSUED:

EXPIRATION DATE:

WITNESS FULL NAME:

PHONE NUMBER:

EMAIL ADDRESS:

WITNESS SIGNATURE:

ADDRESS:

DOCUMENT TYPE:	DATE/TIME NOTARIZED:	DOCUMENT DATE:	FEE CHARGED:

COMMENTS:

RECORD NUMBER: 137

NOTARY LOG

FULL NAME:

PHONE NUMBER:

THUMB PRINT

EMAIL ADDRESS:

SIGNER'S SIGNATURE

ADDRESS:

SERVICE PERFORMED:
- ❏ JURAT
- ❏ OATH
- ❏ ACKNOWLEDGEMENT
- ❏ OTHER: _____

IDENTIFICATION
- ❏ ID CARD
- ❏ PASSPORT
- ❏ DRIVER'S LICENSE
- ❏ OTHER: _____
- ❏ CREDIBLE WITNESS
- ❏ KNOWN PERSONALLY

ID NUMBER:

ISSUED BY:

DATE ISSUED:

EXPIRATION DATE:

WITNESS FULL NAME:

PHONE NUMBER:

EMAIL ADDRESS:

WITNESS SIGNATURE:

ADDRESS:

DOCUMENT TYPE:	DATE/TIME NOTARIZED:	DOCUMENT DATE:	FEE CHARGED:

COMMENTS:

RECORD NUMBER: 138

NOTARY LOG

FULL NAME:	PHONE NUMBER:	THUMB PRINT
EMAIL ADDRESS:	SIGNER'S SIGNATURE	
ADDRESS:		

SERVICE PERFORMED:
- ❏ JURAT
- ❏ OATH
- ❏ ACKNOWLEDGEMENT
- ❏ OTHER: _____

IDENTIFICATION
- ❏ ID CARD
- ❏ PASSPORT
- ❏ DRIVER'S LICENSE
- ❏ OTHER: _____
- ❏ CREDIBLE WITNESS
- ❏ KNOWN PERSONALLY

ID NUMBER:

ISSUED BY:

DATE ISSUED: EXPIRATION DATE:

WITNESS FULL NAME: PHONE NUMBER:

EMAIL ADDRESS:

ADDRESS:

WITNESS SIGNATURE:

DOCUMENT TYPE: DATE/TIME NOTARIZED: DOCUMENT DATE: FEE CHARGED:

COMMENTS: RECORD NUMBER: **139**

NOTARY LOG

FULL NAME:	PHONE NUMBER:	THUMB PRINT
EMAIL ADDRESS:	SIGNER'S SIGNATURE	
ADDRESS:		

SERVICE PERFORMED:
- ❏ JURAT
- ❏ OATH
- ❏ ACKNOWLEDGEMENT
- ❏ OTHER: _____

IDENTIFICATION
- ❏ ID CARD
- ❏ PASSPORT
- ❏ DRIVER'S LICENSE
- ❏ OTHER: _____
- ❏ CREDIBLE WITNESS
- ❏ KNOWN PERSONALLY

ID NUMBER:

ISSUED BY:

DATE ISSUED: EXPIRATION DATE:

WITNESS FULL NAME: PHONE NUMBER:

EMAIL ADDRESS:

ADDRESS:

WITNESS SIGNATURE:

DOCUMENT TYPE: DATE/TIME NOTARIZED: DOCUMENT DATE: FEE CHARGED:

COMMENTS: RECORD NUMBER: **140**

NOTARY LOG

FULL NAME:	PHONE NUMBER:	THUMB PRINT

EMAIL ADDRESS:

SIGNER'S SIGNATURE

ADDRESS:

SERVICE PERFORMED:	IDENTIFICATION	ID NUMBER:
❑ JURAT	❑ ID CARD ❑ CREDIBLE WITNESS	
❑ OATH	❑ PASSPORT ❑ KNOWN PERSONALLY	ISSUED BY:
❑ ACKNOWLEDGEMENT	❑ DRIVER'S LICENSE	
❑ OTHER: _____	❑ OTHER: _____	DATE ISSUED: EXPIRATION DATE:

WITNESS FULL NAME:　　　　　**PHONE NUMBER:**

EMAIL ADDRESS:　　　　　**WITNESS SIGNATURE:**

ADDRESS:

DOCUMENT TYPE:	DATE/TIME NOTARIZED:	DOCUMENT DATE:	FEE CHARGED:

COMMENTS:		RECORD NUMBER: 141

NOTARY LOG

FULL NAME:	PHONE NUMBER:	THUMB PRINT

EMAIL ADDRESS:

SIGNER'S SIGNATURE

ADDRESS:

SERVICE PERFORMED:	IDENTIFICATION	ID NUMBER:
❑ JURAT	❑ ID CARD ❑ CREDIBLE WITNESS	
❑ OATH	❑ PASSPORT ❑ KNOWN PERSONALLY	ISSUED BY:
❑ ACKNOWLEDGEMENT	❑ DRIVER'S LICENSE	
❑ OTHER: _____	❑ OTHER: _____	DATE ISSUED: EXPIRATION DATE:

WITNESS FULL NAME:　　　　　**PHONE NUMBER:**

EMAIL ADDRESS:　　　　　**WITNESS SIGNATURE:**

ADDRESS:

DOCUMENT TYPE:	DATE/TIME NOTARIZED:	DOCUMENT DATE:	FEE CHARGED:

COMMENTS:		RECORD NUMBER: 142

NOTARY LOG

FULL NAME:	PHONE NUMBER:	THUMB PRINT
EMAIL ADDRESS:	SIGNER'S SIGNATURE	
ADDRESS:		

SERVICE PERFORMED:
- ❑ JURAT
- ❑ OATH
- ❑ ACKNOWLEDGEMENT
- ❑ OTHER: _____

IDENTIFICATION
- ❑ ID CARD
- ❑ PASSPORT
- ❑ DRIVER'S LICENSE
- ❑ OTHER: _____
- ❑ CREDIBLE WITNESS
- ❑ KNOWN PERSONALLY

ID NUMBER:

ISSUED BY:

DATE ISSUED: EXPIRATION DATE:

WITNESS FULL NAME:	PHONE NUMBER:
EMAIL ADDRESS:	WITNESS SIGNATURE:
ADDRESS:	

DOCUMENT TYPE:	DATE/TIME NOTARIZED:	DOCUMENT DATE:	FEE CHARGED:

COMMENTS:		RECORD NUMBER: **143**

NOTARY LOG

FULL NAME:	PHONE NUMBER:	THUMB PRINT
EMAIL ADDRESS:	SIGNER'S SIGNATURE	
ADDRESS:		

SERVICE PERFORMED:
- ❑ JURAT
- ❑ OATH
- ❑ ACKNOWLEDGEMENT
- ❑ OTHER: _____

IDENTIFICATION
- ❑ ID CARD
- ❑ PASSPORT
- ❑ DRIVER'S LICENSE
- ❑ OTHER: _____
- ❑ CREDIBLE WITNESS
- ❑ KNOWN PERSONALLY

ID NUMBER:

ISSUED BY:

DATE ISSUED: EXPIRATION DATE:

WITNESS FULL NAME:	PHONE NUMBER:
EMAIL ADDRESS:	WITNESS SIGNATURE:
ADDRESS:	

DOCUMENT TYPE:	DATE/TIME NOTARIZED:	DOCUMENT DATE:	FEE CHARGED:

COMMENTS:	RECORD NUMBER: **144**

NOTARY LOG

FULL NAME:	PHONE NUMBER:	THUMB PRINT
EMAIL ADDRESS:	SIGNER'S SIGNATURE	
ADDRESS:		

SERVICE PERFORMED:
- ❑ JURAT
- ❑ OATH
- ❑ ACKNOWLEDGEMENT
- ❑ OTHER: _____

IDENTIFICATION
- ❑ ID CARD
- ❑ PASSPORT
- ❑ DRIVER'S LICENSE
- ❑ OTHER: _____
- ❑ CREDIBLE WITNESS
- ❑ KNOWN PERSONALLY

ID NUMBER:

ISSUED BY:

DATE ISSUED:

EXPIRATION DATE:

WITNESS FULL NAME:	PHONE NUMBER:
EMAIL ADDRESS:	WITNESS SIGNATURE:
ADDRESS:	

DOCUMENT TYPE:	DATE/TIME NOTARIZED:	DOCUMENT DATE:	FEE CHARGED:

COMMENTS:

RECORD NUMBER: **145**

NOTARY LOG

FULL NAME:	PHONE NUMBER:	THUMB PRINT
EMAIL ADDRESS:	SIGNER'S SIGNATURE	
ADDRESS:		

SERVICE PERFORMED:
- ❑ JURAT
- ❑ OATH
- ❑ ACKNOWLEDGEMENT
- ❑ OTHER: _____

IDENTIFICATION
- ❑ ID CARD
- ❑ PASSPORT
- ❑ DRIVER'S LICENSE
- ❑ OTHER: _____
- ❑ CREDIBLE WITNESS
- ❑ KNOWN PERSONALLY

ID NUMBER:

ISSUED BY:

DATE ISSUED:

EXPIRATION DATE:

WITNESS FULL NAME:	PHONE NUMBER:
EMAIL ADDRESS:	WITNESS SIGNATURE:
ADDRESS:	

DOCUMENT TYPE:	DATE/TIME NOTARIZED:	DOCUMENT DATE:	FEE CHARGED:

COMMENTS:

RECORD NUMBER: **146**

NOTARY LOG

FULL NAME:	PHONE NUMBER:	THUMB PRINT
EMAIL ADDRESS:	SIGNER'S SIGNATURE	
ADDRESS:		

SERVICE PERFORMED:	IDENTIFICATION	ID NUMBER:
❏ JURAT	❏ ID CARD ❏ CREDIBLE WITNESS	
❏ OATH	❏ PASSPORT ❏ KNOWN PERSONALLY	ISSUED BY:
❏ ACKNOWLEDGEMENT	❏ DRIVER'S LICENSE	
❏ OTHER: _____	❏ OTHER: _____	DATE ISSUED: / EXPIRATION DATE:

WITNESS FULL NAME:	PHONE NUMBER:
EMAIL ADDRESS:	WITNESS SIGNATURE:
ADDRESS:	

DOCUMENT TYPE:	DATE/TIME NOTARIZED:	DOCUMENT DATE:	FEE CHARGED:
COMMENTS:			RECORD NUMBER: **147**

NOTARY LOG

FULL NAME:	PHONE NUMBER:	THUMB PRINT
EMAIL ADDRESS:	SIGNER'S SIGNATURE	
ADDRESS:		

SERVICE PERFORMED:	IDENTIFICATION	ID NUMBER:
❏ JURAT	❏ ID CARD ❏ CREDIBLE WITNESS	
❏ OATH	❏ PASSPORT ❏ KNOWN PERSONALLY	ISSUED BY:
❏ ACKNOWLEDGEMENT	❏ DRIVER'S LICENSE	
❏ OTHER: _____	❏ OTHER: _____	DATE ISSUED: / EXPIRATION DATE:

WITNESS FULL NAME:	PHONE NUMBER:
EMAIL ADDRESS:	WITNESS SIGNATURE:
ADDRESS:	

DOCUMENT TYPE:	DATE/TIME NOTARIZED:	DOCUMENT DATE:	FEE CHARGED:
COMMENTS:			RECORD NUMBER: **148**

NOTARY LOG

FULL NAME:	PHONE NUMBER:	THUMB PRINT
EMAIL ADDRESS:	SIGNER'S SIGNATURE	
ADDRESS:		

SERVICE PERFORMED:	IDENTIFICATION		ID NUMBER:
❑ JURAT	❑ ID CARD	❑ CREDIBLE WITNESS	
❑ OATH	❑ PASSPORT	❑ KNOWN PERSONALLY	ISSUED BY:
❑ ACKNOWLEDGEMENT	❑ DRIVER'S LICENSE		
❑ OTHER: _____	❑ OTHER: _____		DATE ISSUED: EXPIRATION DATE:

WITNESS FULL NAME:	PHONE NUMBER:
EMAIL ADDRESS:	WITNESS SIGNATURE:
ADDRESS:	

DOCUMENT TYPE:	DATE/TIME NOTARIZED:	DOCUMENT DATE:	FEE CHARGED:
COMMENTS:			RECORD NUMBER: **149**

NOTARY LOG

FULL NAME:	PHONE NUMBER:	THUMB PRINT
EMAIL ADDRESS:	SIGNER'S SIGNATURE	
ADDRESS:		

SERVICE PERFORMED:	IDENTIFICATION		ID NUMBER:
❑ JURAT	❑ ID CARD	❑ CREDIBLE WITNESS	
❑ OATH	❑ PASSPORT	❑ KNOWN PERSONALLY	ISSUED BY:
❑ ACKNOWLEDGEMENT	❑ DRIVER'S LICENSE		
❑ OTHER: _____	❑ OTHER: _____		DATE ISSUED: EXPIRATION DATE:

WITNESS FULL NAME:	PHONE NUMBER:
EMAIL ADDRESS:	WITNESS SIGNATURE:
ADDRESS:	

DOCUMENT TYPE:	DATE/TIME NOTARIZED:	DOCUMENT DATE:	FEE CHARGED:
COMMENTS:			RECORD NUMBER: **150**

NOTARY LOG

FULL NAME:	PHONE NUMBER:
EMAIL ADDRESS:	SIGNER'S SIGNATURE
ADDRESS:	

THUMB PRINT

SERVICE PERFORMED:
- ❏ JURAT
- ❏ OATH
- ❏ ACKNOWLEDGEMENT
- ❏ OTHER: _____

IDENTIFICATION
- ❏ ID CARD
- ❏ PASSPORT
- ❏ DRIVER'S LICENSE
- ❏ OTHER: _____
- ❏ CREDIBLE WITNESS
- ❏ KNOWN PERSONALLY

ID NUMBER:

ISSUED BY:

DATE ISSUED: | EXPIRATION DATE:

WITNESS FULL NAME:	PHONE NUMBER:
EMAIL ADDRESS:	WITNESS SIGNATURE:
ADDRESS:	

DOCUMENT TYPE:	DATE/TIME NOTARIZED:	DOCUMENT DATE:	FEE CHARGED:

COMMENTS:

RECORD NUMBER: **151**

NOTARY LOG

FULL NAME:	PHONE NUMBER:
EMAIL ADDRESS:	SIGNER'S SIGNATURE
ADDRESS:	

THUMB PRINT

SERVICE PERFORMED:
- ❏ JURAT
- ❏ OATH
- ❏ ACKNOWLEDGEMENT
- ❏ OTHER: _____

IDENTIFICATION
- ❏ ID CARD
- ❏ PASSPORT
- ❏ DRIVER'S LICENSE
- ❏ OTHER: _____
- ❏ CREDIBLE WITNESS
- ❏ KNOWN PERSONALLY

ID NUMBER:

ISSUED BY:

DATE ISSUED: | EXPIRATION DATE:

WITNESS FULL NAME:	PHONE NUMBER:
EMAIL ADDRESS:	WITNESS SIGNATURE:
ADDRESS:	

DOCUMENT TYPE:	DATE/TIME NOTARIZED:	DOCUMENT DATE:	FEE CHARGED:

COMMENTS:

RECORD NUMBER: **152**

NOTARY LOG

FULL NAME:	PHONE NUMBER:	THUMB PRINT
EMAIL ADDRESS:	SIGNER'S SIGNATURE	
ADDRESS:		

SERVICE PERFORMED:
- ❑ JURAT
- ❑ OATH
- ❑ ACKNOWLEDGEMENT
- ❑ OTHER: _____

IDENTIFICATION
- ❑ ID CARD
- ❑ PASSPORT
- ❑ DRIVER'S LICENSE
- ❑ OTHER: _____
- ❑ CREDIBLE WITNESS
- ❑ KNOWN PERSONALLY

ID NUMBER:

ISSUED BY:

DATE ISSUED: EXPIRATION DATE:

WITNESS FULL NAME:	PHONE NUMBER:
EMAIL ADDRESS:	WITNESS SIGNATURE:
ADDRESS:	

DOCUMENT TYPE:	DATE/TIME NOTARIZED:	DOCUMENT DATE:	FEE CHARGED:

COMMENTS:

RECORD NUMBER: **153**

NOTARY LOG

FULL NAME:	PHONE NUMBER:	THUMB PRINT
EMAIL ADDRESS:	SIGNER'S SIGNATURE	
ADDRESS:		

SERVICE PERFORMED:
- ❑ JURAT
- ❑ OATH
- ❑ ACKNOWLEDGEMENT
- ❑ OTHER: _____

IDENTIFICATION
- ❑ ID CARD
- ❑ PASSPORT
- ❑ DRIVER'S LICENSE
- ❑ OTHER: _____
- ❑ CREDIBLE WITNESS
- ❑ KNOWN PERSONALLY

ID NUMBER:

ISSUED BY:

DATE ISSUED: EXPIRATION DATE:

WITNESS FULL NAME:	PHONE NUMBER:
EMAIL ADDRESS:	WITNESS SIGNATURE:
ADDRESS:	

DOCUMENT TYPE:	DATE/TIME NOTARIZED:	DOCUMENT DATE:	FEE CHARGED:

COMMENTS:

RECORD NUMBER: **154**

NOTARY LOG

		THUMB PRINT
FULL NAME:	**PHONE NUMBER:**	
EMAIL ADDRESS:	**SIGNER'S SIGNATURE**	
ADDRESS:		

SERVICE PERFORMED:
- ❑ JURAT
- ❑ OATH
- ❑ ACKNOWLEDGEMENT
- ❑ OTHER: _____

IDENTIFICATION
- ❑ ID CARD
- ❑ PASSPORT
- ❑ DRIVER'S LICENSE
- ❑ OTHER: _____
- ❑ CREDIBLE WITNESS
- ❑ KNOWN PERSONALLY

ID NUMBER:

ISSUED BY:

DATE ISSUED: | **EXPIRATION DATE:**

WITNESS FULL NAME:	**PHONE NUMBER:**
EMAIL ADDRESS:	**WITNESS SIGNATURE:**
ADDRESS:	

DOCUMENT TYPE:	DATE/TIME NOTARIZED:	DOCUMENT DATE:	FEE CHARGED:

COMMENTS: | **RECORD NUMBER:** 155

NOTARY LOG

		THUMB PRINT
FULL NAME:	**PHONE NUMBER:**	
EMAIL ADDRESS:	**SIGNER'S SIGNATURE**	
ADDRESS:		

SERVICE PERFORMED:
- ❑ JURAT
- ❑ OATH
- ❑ ACKNOWLEDGEMENT
- ❑ OTHER: _____

IDENTIFICATION
- ❑ ID CARD
- ❑ PASSPORT
- ❑ DRIVER'S LICENSE
- ❑ OTHER: _____
- ❑ CREDIBLE WITNESS
- ❑ KNOWN PERSONALLY

ID NUMBER:

ISSUED BY:

DATE ISSUED: | **EXPIRATION DATE:**

WITNESS FULL NAME:	**PHONE NUMBER:**
EMAIL ADDRESS:	**WITNESS SIGNATURE:**
ADDRESS:	

DOCUMENT TYPE:	DATE/TIME NOTARIZED:	DOCUMENT DATE:	FEE CHARGED:

COMMENTS: | **RECORD NUMBER:** 156

NOTARY LOG

FULL NAME:	PHONE NUMBER:	THUMB PRINT
EMAIL ADDRESS:	SIGNER'S SIGNATURE	
ADDRESS:		

SERVICE PERFORMED:	IDENTIFICATION	ID NUMBER:
❏ JURAT	❏ ID CARD ❏ CREDIBLE WITNESS	
❏ OATH	❏ PASSPORT ❏ KNOWN PERSONALLY	ISSUED BY:
❏ ACKNOWLEDGEMENT	❏ DRIVER'S LICENSE	DATE ISSUED: EXPIRATION DATE:
❏ OTHER: _____	❏ OTHER: _____	

WITNESS FULL NAME:	PHONE NUMBER:
EMAIL ADDRESS:	WITNESS SIGNATURE:
ADDRESS:	

DOCUMENT TYPE:	DATE/TIME NOTARIZED:	DOCUMENT DATE:	FEE CHARGED:

COMMENTS:		RECORD NUMBER: 157

NOTARY LOG

FULL NAME:	PHONE NUMBER:	THUMB PRINT
EMAIL ADDRESS:	SIGNER'S SIGNATURE	
ADDRESS:		

SERVICE PERFORMED:	IDENTIFICATION	ID NUMBER:
❏ JURAT	❏ ID CARD ❏ CREDIBLE WITNESS	
❏ OATH	❏ PASSPORT ❏ KNOWN PERSONALLY	ISSUED BY:
❏ ACKNOWLEDGEMENT	❏ DRIVER'S LICENSE	DATE ISSUED: EXPIRATION DATE:
❏ OTHER: _____	❏ OTHER: _____	

WITNESS FULL NAME:	PHONE NUMBER:
EMAIL ADDRESS:	WITNESS SIGNATURE:
ADDRESS:	

DOCUMENT TYPE:	DATE/TIME NOTARIZED:	DOCUMENT DATE:	FEE CHARGED:

COMMENTS:		RECORD NUMBER: 158

NOTARY LOG

FULL NAME:	PHONE NUMBER:	THUMB PRINT
EMAIL ADDRESS:	SIGNER'S SIGNATURE	
ADDRESS:		

SERVICE PERFORMED:
- ❏ JURAT
- ❏ OATH
- ❏ ACKNOWLEDGEMENT
- ❏ OTHER: _____

IDENTIFICATION
- ❏ ID CARD
- ❏ PASSPORT
- ❏ DRIVER'S LICENSE
- ❏ OTHER: _____
- ❏ CREDIBLE WITNESS
- ❏ KNOWN PERSONALLY

ID NUMBER:

ISSUED BY:

DATE ISSUED: | EXPIRATION DATE:

WITNESS FULL NAME:	PHONE NUMBER:
EMAIL ADDRESS:	WITNESS SIGNATURE:
ADDRESS:	

DOCUMENT TYPE:	DATE/TIME NOTARIZED:	DOCUMENT DATE:	FEE CHARGED:

COMMENTS:

RECORD NUMBER: **159**

NOTARY LOG

FULL NAME:	PHONE NUMBER:	THUMB PRINT
EMAIL ADDRESS:	SIGNER'S SIGNATURE	
ADDRESS:		

SERVICE PERFORMED:
- ❏ JURAT
- ❏ OATH
- ❏ ACKNOWLEDGEMENT
- ❏ OTHER: _____

IDENTIFICATION
- ❏ ID CARD
- ❏ PASSPORT
- ❏ DRIVER'S LICENSE
- ❏ OTHER: _____
- ❏ CREDIBLE WITNESS
- ❏ KNOWN PERSONALLY

ID NUMBER:

ISSUED BY:

DATE ISSUED: | EXPIRATION DATE:

WITNESS FULL NAME:	PHONE NUMBER:
EMAIL ADDRESS:	WITNESS SIGNATURE:
ADDRESS:	

DOCUMENT TYPE:	DATE/TIME NOTARIZED:	DOCUMENT DATE:	FEE CHARGED:

COMMENTS:

RECORD NUMBER: **160**

NOTARY LOG

FULL NAME:		PHONE NUMBER:	THUMB PRINT
EMAIL ADDRESS:		SIGNER'S SIGNATURE	
ADDRESS:			

SERVICE PERFORMED:
- ❏ JURAT
- ❏ OATH
- ❏ ACKNOWLEDGEMENT
- ❏ OTHER: _____

IDENTIFICATION
- ❏ ID CARD
- ❏ PASSPORT
- ❏ DRIVER'S LICENSE
- ❏ OTHER: _____
- ❏ CREDIBLE WITNESS
- ❏ KNOWN PERSONALLY

ID NUMBER:

ISSUED BY:

DATE ISSUED: EXPIRATION DATE:

WITNESS FULL NAME:	PHONE NUMBER:
EMAIL ADDRESS:	WITNESS SIGNATURE:
ADDRESS:	

DOCUMENT TYPE:	DATE/TIME NOTARIZED:	DOCUMENT DATE:	FEE CHARGED:
COMMENTS:			RECORD NUMBER: **161**

NOTARY LOG

FULL NAME:		PHONE NUMBER:	THUMB PRINT
EMAIL ADDRESS:		SIGNER'S SIGNATURE	
ADDRESS:			

SERVICE PERFORMED:
- ❏ JURAT
- ❏ OATH
- ❏ ACKNOWLEDGEMENT
- ❏ OTHER: _____

IDENTIFICATION
- ❏ ID CARD
- ❏ PASSPORT
- ❏ DRIVER'S LICENSE
- ❏ OTHER: _____
- ❏ CREDIBLE WITNESS
- ❏ KNOWN PERSONALLY

ID NUMBER:

ISSUED BY:

DATE ISSUED: EXPIRATION DATE:

WITNESS FULL NAME:	PHONE NUMBER:
EMAIL ADDRESS:	WITNESS SIGNATURE:
ADDRESS:	

DOCUMENT TYPE:	DATE/TIME NOTARIZED:	DOCUMENT DATE:	FEE CHARGED:
COMMENTS:			RECORD NUMBER: **162**

NOTARY LOG

FULL NAME:	PHONE NUMBER:	THUMB PRINT
EMAIL ADDRESS:	SIGNER'S SIGNATURE	
ADDRESS:		

SERVICE PERFORMED:
- ❏ JURAT
- ❏ OATH
- ❏ ACKNOWLEDGEMENT
- ❏ OTHER: _____

IDENTIFICATION
- ❏ ID CARD
- ❏ PASSPORT
- ❏ DRIVER'S LICENSE
- ❏ OTHER: _____
- ❏ CREDIBLE WITNESS
- ❏ KNOWN PERSONALLY

ID NUMBER:

ISSUED BY:

DATE ISSUED: EXPIRATION DATE:

WITNESS FULL NAME:	PHONE NUMBER:
EMAIL ADDRESS:	WITNESS SIGNATURE:
ADDRESS:	

DOCUMENT TYPE:	DATE/TIME NOTARIZED:	DOCUMENT DATE:	FEE CHARGED:

COMMENTS: RECORD NUMBER: **163**

NOTARY LOG

FULL NAME:	PHONE NUMBER:	THUMB PRINT
EMAIL ADDRESS:	SIGNER'S SIGNATURE	
ADDRESS:		

SERVICE PERFORMED:
- ❏ JURAT
- ❏ OATH
- ❏ ACKNOWLEDGEMENT
- ❏ OTHER: _____

IDENTIFICATION
- ❏ ID CARD
- ❏ PASSPORT
- ❏ DRIVER'S LICENSE
- ❏ OTHER: _____
- ❏ CREDIBLE WITNESS
- ❏ KNOWN PERSONALLY

ID NUMBER:

ISSUED BY:

DATE ISSUED: EXPIRATION DATE:

WITNESS FULL NAME:	PHONE NUMBER:
EMAIL ADDRESS:	WITNESS SIGNATURE:
ADDRESS:	

DOCUMENT TYPE:	DATE/TIME NOTARIZED:	DOCUMENT DATE:	FEE CHARGED:

COMMENTS: RECORD NUMBER: **164**

NOTARY LOG

FULL NAME:

PHONE NUMBER:

THUMB PRINT

EMAIL ADDRESS:

SIGNER'S SIGNATURE

ADDRESS:

SERVICE PERFORMED:
- ❑ JURAT
- ❑ OATH
- ❑ ACKNOWLEDGEMENT
- ❑ OTHER: _____

IDENTIFICATION
- ❑ ID CARD
- ❑ PASSPORT
- ❑ DRIVER'S LICENSE
- ❑ OTHER: _____
- ❑ CREDIBLE WITNESS
- ❑ KNOWN PERSONALLY

ID NUMBER:

ISSUED BY:

DATE ISSUED:

EXPIRATION DATE:

WITNESS FULL NAME:

PHONE NUMBER:

EMAIL ADDRESS:

WITNESS SIGNATURE:

ADDRESS:

DOCUMENT TYPE:

DATE/TIME NOTARIZED:

DOCUMENT DATE:

FEE CHARGED:

COMMENTS:

RECORD NUMBER: 165

NOTARY LOG

FULL NAME:

PHONE NUMBER:

THUMB PRINT

EMAIL ADDRESS:

SIGNER'S SIGNATURE

ADDRESS:

SERVICE PERFORMED:
- ❑ JURAT
- ❑ OATH
- ❑ ACKNOWLEDGEMENT
- ❑ OTHER: _____

IDENTIFICATION
- ❑ ID CARD
- ❑ PASSPORT
- ❑ DRIVER'S LICENSE
- ❑ OTHER: _____
- ❑ CREDIBLE WITNESS
- ❑ KNOWN PERSONALLY

ID NUMBER:

ISSUED BY:

DATE ISSUED:

EXPIRATION DATE:

WITNESS FULL NAME:

PHONE NUMBER:

EMAIL ADDRESS:

WITNESS SIGNATURE:

ADDRESS:

DOCUMENT TYPE:

DATE/TIME NOTARIZED:

DOCUMENT DATE:

FEE CHARGED:

COMMENTS:

RECORD NUMBER: 166

NOTARY LOG

FULL NAME:	PHONE NUMBER:	THUMB PRINT
EMAIL ADDRESS:	SIGNER'S SIGNATURE	
ADDRESS:		

SERVICE PERFORMED:
- ❏ JURAT
- ❏ OATH
- ❏ ACKNOWLEDGEMENT
- ❏ OTHER: _____

IDENTIFICATION
- ❏ ID CARD
- ❏ PASSPORT
- ❏ DRIVER'S LICENSE
- ❏ OTHER: _____
- ❏ CREDIBLE WITNESS
- ❏ KNOWN PERSONALLY

ID NUMBER:

ISSUED BY:

DATE ISSUED: EXPIRATION DATE:

WITNESS FULL NAME:	PHONE NUMBER:
EMAIL ADDRESS:	WITNESS SIGNATURE:
ADDRESS:	

DOCUMENT TYPE:	DATE/TIME NOTARIZED:	DOCUMENT DATE:	FEE CHARGED:

COMMENTS:		RECORD NUMBER: **167**

NOTARY LOG

FULL NAME:	PHONE NUMBER:	THUMB PRINT
EMAIL ADDRESS:	SIGNER'S SIGNATURE	
ADDRESS:		

SERVICE PERFORMED:
- ❏ JURAT
- ❏ OATH
- ❏ ACKNOWLEDGEMENT
- ❏ OTHER: _____

IDENTIFICATION
- ❏ ID CARD
- ❏ PASSPORT
- ❏ DRIVER'S LICENSE
- ❏ OTHER: _____
- ❏ CREDIBLE WITNESS
- ❏ KNOWN PERSONALLY

ID NUMBER:

ISSUED BY:

DATE ISSUED: EXPIRATION DATE:

WITNESS FULL NAME:	PHONE NUMBER:
EMAIL ADDRESS:	WITNESS SIGNATURE:
ADDRESS:	

DOCUMENT TYPE:	DATE/TIME NOTARIZED:	DOCUMENT DATE:	FEE CHARGED:

COMMENTS:		RECORD NUMBER: **168**

NOTARY LOG

FULL NAME:	PHONE NUMBER:	THUMB PRINT
EMAIL ADDRESS:	SIGNER'S SIGNATURE	
ADDRESS:		

SERVICE PERFORMED:
- ❑ JURAT
- ❑ OATH
- ❑ ACKNOWLEDGEMENT
- ❑ OTHER: _____

IDENTIFICATION
- ❑ ID CARD
- ❑ PASSPORT
- ❑ DRIVER'S LICENSE
- ❑ OTHER: _____
- ❑ CREDIBLE WITNESS
- ❑ KNOWN PERSONALLY

ID NUMBER:

ISSUED BY:

DATE ISSUED: EXPIRATION DATE:

WITNESS FULL NAME:	PHONE NUMBER:
EMAIL ADDRESS:	WITNESS SIGNATURE:
ADDRESS:	

DOCUMENT TYPE:	DATE/TIME NOTARIZED:	DOCUMENT DATE:	FEE CHARGED:

COMMENTS:		RECORD NUMBER: **169**

NOTARY LOG

FULL NAME:	PHONE NUMBER:	THUMB PRINT
EMAIL ADDRESS:	SIGNER'S SIGNATURE	
ADDRESS:		

SERVICE PERFORMED:
- ❑ JURAT
- ❑ OATH
- ❑ ACKNOWLEDGEMENT
- ❑ OTHER: _____

IDENTIFICATION
- ❑ ID CARD
- ❑ PASSPORT
- ❑ DRIVER'S LICENSE
- ❑ OTHER: _____
- ❑ CREDIBLE WITNESS
- ❑ KNOWN PERSONALLY

ID NUMBER:

ISSUED BY:

DATE ISSUED: EXPIRATION DATE:

WITNESS FULL NAME:	PHONE NUMBER:
EMAIL ADDRESS:	WITNESS SIGNATURE:
ADDRESS:	

DOCUMENT TYPE:	DATE/TIME NOTARIZED:	DOCUMENT DATE:	FEE CHARGED:

COMMENTS:		RECORD NUMBER: **170**

NOTARY LOG

FULL NAME:

PHONE NUMBER:

THUMB PRINT

EMAIL ADDRESS:

SIGNER'S SIGNATURE

ADDRESS:

SERVICE PERFORMED:
- ❏ JURAT
- ❏ OATH
- ❏ ACKNOWLEDGEMENT
- ❏ OTHER: _____

IDENTIFICATION
- ❏ ID CARD
- ❏ PASSPORT
- ❏ DRIVER'S LICENSE
- ❏ OTHER: _____
- ❏ CREDIBLE WITNESS
- ❏ KNOWN PERSONALLY

ID NUMBER:

ISSUED BY:

DATE ISSUED:

EXPIRATION DATE:

WITNESS FULL NAME:

PHONE NUMBER:

EMAIL ADDRESS:

WITNESS SIGNATURE:

ADDRESS:

DOCUMENT TYPE:

DATE/TIME NOTARIZED:

DOCUMENT DATE:

FEE CHARGED:

COMMENTS:

RECORD NUMBER: 171

NOTARY LOG

FULL NAME:

PHONE NUMBER:

THUMB PRINT

EMAIL ADDRESS:

SIGNER'S SIGNATURE

ADDRESS:

SERVICE PERFORMED:
- ❏ JURAT
- ❏ OATH
- ❏ ACKNOWLEDGEMENT
- ❏ OTHER: _____

IDENTIFICATION
- ❏ ID CARD
- ❏ PASSPORT
- ❏ DRIVER'S LICENSE
- ❏ OTHER: _____
- ❏ CREDIBLE WITNESS
- ❏ KNOWN PERSONALLY

ID NUMBER:

ISSUED BY:

DATE ISSUED:

EXPIRATION DATE:

WITNESS FULL NAME:

PHONE NUMBER:

EMAIL ADDRESS:

WITNESS SIGNATURE:

ADDRESS:

DOCUMENT TYPE:

DATE/TIME NOTARIZED:

DOCUMENT DATE:

FEE CHARGED:

COMMENTS:

RECORD NUMBER: 172

NOTARY LOG

FULL NAME:	PHONE NUMBER:	THUMB PRINT
EMAIL ADDRESS:	SIGNER'S SIGNATURE	
ADDRESS:		

SERVICE PERFORMED:	IDENTIFICATION		ID NUMBER:
❑ JURAT	❑ ID CARD	❑ CREDIBLE WITNESS	
❑ OATH	❑ PASSPORT	❑ KNOWN PERSONALLY	ISSUED BY:
❑ ACKNOWLEDGEMENT	❑ DRIVER'S LICENSE		
❑ OTHER: _____	❑ OTHER: _____		DATE ISSUED: / EXPIRATION DATE:

WITNESS FULL NAME:	PHONE NUMBER:
EMAIL ADDRESS:	WITNESS SIGNATURE:
ADDRESS:	

DOCUMENT TYPE:	DATE/TIME NOTARIZED:	DOCUMENT DATE:	FEE CHARGED:

COMMENTS:		RECORD NUMBER: **173**

NOTARY LOG

FULL NAME:	PHONE NUMBER:	THUMB PRINT
EMAIL ADDRESS:	SIGNER'S SIGNATURE	
ADDRESS:		

SERVICE PERFORMED:	IDENTIFICATION		ID NUMBER:
❑ JURAT	❑ ID CARD	❑ CREDIBLE WITNESS	
❑ OATH	❑ PASSPORT	❑ KNOWN PERSONALLY	ISSUED BY:
❑ ACKNOWLEDGEMENT	❑ DRIVER'S LICENSE		
❑ OTHER: _____	❑ OTHER: _____		DATE ISSUED: / EXPIRATION DATE:

WITNESS FULL NAME:	PHONE NUMBER:
EMAIL ADDRESS:	WITNESS SIGNATURE:
ADDRESS:	

DOCUMENT TYPE:	DATE/TIME NOTARIZED:	DOCUMENT DATE:	FEE CHARGED:

COMMENTS:		RECORD NUMBER: **174**

NOTARY LOG

FULL NAME:

PHONE NUMBER:

THUMB PRINT

EMAIL ADDRESS:

SIGNER'S SIGNATURE

ADDRESS:

SERVICE PERFORMED:

- ❑ JURAT
- ❑ OATH
- ❑ ACKNOWLEDGEMENT
- ❑ OTHER: _____

IDENTIFICATION

- ❑ ID CARD
- ❑ PASSPORT
- ❑ DRIVER'S LICENSE
- ❑ OTHER: _____
- ❑ CREDIBLE WITNESS
- ❑ KNOWN PERSONALLY

ID NUMBER:

ISSUED BY:

DATE ISSUED:

EXPIRATION DATE:

WITNESS FULL NAME:

PHONE NUMBER:

EMAIL ADDRESS:

WITNESS SIGNATURE:

ADDRESS:

DOCUMENT TYPE:	DATE/TIME NOTARIZED:	DOCUMENT DATE:	FEE CHARGED:

COMMENTS:

RECORD NUMBER: 175

NOTARY LOG

FULL NAME:

PHONE NUMBER:

THUMB PRINT

EMAIL ADDRESS:

SIGNER'S SIGNATURE

ADDRESS:

SERVICE PERFORMED:

- ❑ JURAT
- ❑ OATH
- ❑ ACKNOWLEDGEMENT
- ❑ OTHER: _____

IDENTIFICATION

- ❑ ID CARD
- ❑ PASSPORT
- ❑ DRIVER'S LICENSE
- ❑ OTHER: _____
- ❑ CREDIBLE WITNESS
- ❑ KNOWN PERSONALLY

ID NUMBER:

ISSUED BY:

DATE ISSUED:

EXPIRATION DATE:

WITNESS FULL NAME:

PHONE NUMBER:

EMAIL ADDRESS:

WITNESS SIGNATURE:

ADDRESS:

DOCUMENT TYPE:	DATE/TIME NOTARIZED:	DOCUMENT DATE:	FEE CHARGED:

COMMENTS:

RECORD NUMBER: 176

NOTARY LOG

FULL NAME:	PHONE NUMBER:	THUMB PRINT

EMAIL ADDRESS:

ADDRESS:

SIGNER'S SIGNATURE

SERVICE PERFORMED:	IDENTIFICATION	ID NUMBER:
❏ JURAT	❏ ID CARD ❏ CREDIBLE WITNESS	
❏ OATH	❏ PASSPORT ❏ KNOWN PERSONALLY	ISSUED BY:
❏ ACKNOWLEDGEMENT	❏ DRIVER'S LICENSE	
❏ OTHER: _____	❏ OTHER: _____	DATE ISSUED: / EXPIRATION DATE:

WITNESS FULL NAME: **PHONE NUMBER:**

EMAIL ADDRESS: **WITNESS SIGNATURE:**

ADDRESS:

DOCUMENT TYPE:	DATE/TIME NOTARIZED:	DOCUMENT DATE:	FEE CHARGED:

COMMENTS: **RECORD NUMBER: 177**

NOTARY LOG

FULL NAME:	PHONE NUMBER:	THUMB PRINT

EMAIL ADDRESS:

ADDRESS:

SIGNER'S SIGNATURE

SERVICE PERFORMED:	IDENTIFICATION	ID NUMBER:
❏ JURAT	❏ ID CARD ❏ CREDIBLE WITNESS	
❏ OATH	❏ PASSPORT ❏ KNOWN PERSONALLY	ISSUED BY:
❏ ACKNOWLEDGEMENT	❏ DRIVER'S LICENSE	
❏ OTHER: _____	❏ OTHER: _____	DATE ISSUED: / EXPIRATION DATE:

WITNESS FULL NAME: **PHONE NUMBER:**

EMAIL ADDRESS: **WITNESS SIGNATURE:**

ADDRESS:

DOCUMENT TYPE:	DATE/TIME NOTARIZED:	DOCUMENT DATE:	FEE CHARGED:

COMMENTS: **RECORD NUMBER: 178**

NOTARY LOG

FULL NAME:

PHONE NUMBER:

THUMB PRINT

EMAIL ADDRESS:

SIGNER'S SIGNATURE

ADDRESS:

SERVICE PERFORMED:
- ❑ JURAT
- ❑ OATH
- ❑ ACKNOWLEDGEMENT
- ❑ OTHER: _____

IDENTIFICATION
- ❑ ID CARD
- ❑ PASSPORT
- ❑ DRIVER'S LICENSE
- ❑ OTHER: _____
- ❑ CREDIBLE WITNESS
- ❑ KNOWN PERSONALLY

ID NUMBER:

ISSUED BY:

DATE ISSUED:

EXPIRATION DATE:

WITNESS FULL NAME:

PHONE NUMBER:

EMAIL ADDRESS:

WITNESS SIGNATURE:

ADDRESS:

DOCUMENT TYPE:	DATE/TIME NOTARIZED:	DOCUMENT DATE:	FEE CHARGED:

COMMENTS:

RECORD NUMBER: 179

NOTARY LOG

FULL NAME:

PHONE NUMBER:

THUMB PRINT

EMAIL ADDRESS:

SIGNER'S SIGNATURE

ADDRESS:

SERVICE PERFORMED:
- ❑ JURAT
- ❑ OATH
- ❑ ACKNOWLEDGEMENT
- ❑ OTHER: _____

IDENTIFICATION
- ❑ ID CARD
- ❑ PASSPORT
- ❑ DRIVER'S LICENSE
- ❑ OTHER: _____
- ❑ CREDIBLE WITNESS
- ❑ KNOWN PERSONALLY

ID NUMBER:

ISSUED BY:

DATE ISSUED:

EXPIRATION DATE:

WITNESS FULL NAME:

PHONE NUMBER:

EMAIL ADDRESS:

WITNESS SIGNATURE:

ADDRESS:

DOCUMENT TYPE:	DATE/TIME NOTARIZED:	DOCUMENT DATE:	FEE CHARGED:

COMMENTS:

RECORD NUMBER: 180

NOTARY LOG

FULL NAME:	PHONE NUMBER:	THUMB PRINT
EMAIL ADDRESS:	SIGNER'S SIGNATURE	
ADDRESS:		

SERVICE PERFORMED:
- ❑ JURAT
- ❑ OATH
- ❑ ACKNOWLEDGEMENT
- ❑ OTHER: _____

IDENTIFICATION
- ❑ ID CARD
- ❑ PASSPORT
- ❑ DRIVER'S LICENSE
- ❑ OTHER: _____
- ❑ CREDIBLE WITNESS
- ❑ KNOWN PERSONALLY

ID NUMBER:

ISSUED BY:

DATE ISSUED: EXPIRATION DATE:

WITNESS FULL NAME:	PHONE NUMBER:
EMAIL ADDRESS:	WITNESS SIGNATURE:
ADDRESS:	

DOCUMENT TYPE:	DATE/TIME NOTARIZED:	DOCUMENT DATE:	FEE CHARGED:

COMMENTS: RECORD NUMBER: **181**

NOTARY LOG

FULL NAME:	PHONE NUMBER:	THUMB PRINT
EMAIL ADDRESS:	SIGNER'S SIGNATURE	
ADDRESS:		

SERVICE PERFORMED:
- ❑ JURAT
- ❑ OATH
- ❑ ACKNOWLEDGEMENT
- ❑ OTHER: _____

IDENTIFICATION
- ❑ ID CARD
- ❑ PASSPORT
- ❑ DRIVER'S LICENSE
- ❑ OTHER: _____
- ❑ CREDIBLE WITNESS
- ❑ KNOWN PERSONALLY

ID NUMBER:

ISSUED BY:

DATE ISSUED: EXPIRATION DATE:

WITNESS FULL NAME:	PHONE NUMBER:
EMAIL ADDRESS:	WITNESS SIGNATURE:
ADDRESS:	

DOCUMENT TYPE:	DATE/TIME NOTARIZED:	DOCUMENT DATE:	FEE CHARGED:

COMMENTS: RECORD NUMBER: **182**

NOTARY LOG

FULL NAME:

PHONE NUMBER:

THUMB PRINT

EMAIL ADDRESS:

SIGNER'S SIGNATURE

ADDRESS:

SERVICE PERFORMED:
- ❑ JURAT
- ❑ OATH
- ❑ ACKNOWLEDGEMENT
- ❑ OTHER: _____

IDENTIFICATION
- ❑ ID CARD
- ❑ PASSPORT
- ❑ DRIVER'S LICENSE
- ❑ OTHER: _____
- ❑ CREDIBLE WITNESS
- ❑ KNOWN PERSONALLY

ID NUMBER:

ISSUED BY:

DATE ISSUED:

EXPIRATION DATE:

WITNESS FULL NAME:

PHONE NUMBER:

EMAIL ADDRESS:

WITNESS SIGNATURE:

ADDRESS:

DOCUMENT TYPE:

DATE/TIME NOTARIZED:

DOCUMENT DATE:

FEE CHARGED:

COMMENTS:

RECORD NUMBER: 183

NOTARY LOG

FULL NAME:

PHONE NUMBER:

THUMB PRINT

EMAIL ADDRESS:

SIGNER'S SIGNATURE

ADDRESS:

SERVICE PERFORMED:
- ❑ JURAT
- ❑ OATH
- ❑ ACKNOWLEDGEMENT
- ❑ OTHER: _____

IDENTIFICATION
- ❑ ID CARD
- ❑ PASSPORT
- ❑ DRIVER'S LICENSE
- ❑ OTHER: _____
- ❑ CREDIBLE WITNESS
- ❑ KNOWN PERSONALLY

ID NUMBER:

ISSUED BY:

DATE ISSUED:

EXPIRATION DATE:

WITNESS FULL NAME:

PHONE NUMBER:

EMAIL ADDRESS:

WITNESS SIGNATURE:

ADDRESS:

DOCUMENT TYPE:

DATE/TIME NOTARIZED:

DOCUMENT DATE:

FEE CHARGED:

COMMENTS:

RECORD NUMBER: 184

NOTARY LOG

FULL NAME:	PHONE NUMBER:	THUMB PRINT
EMAIL ADDRESS:	SIGNER'S SIGNATURE	
ADDRESS:		

SERVICE PERFORMED:
- ❑ JURAT
- ❑ OATH
- ❑ ACKNOWLEDGEMENT
- ❑ OTHER: _____

IDENTIFICATION
- ❑ ID CARD
- ❑ PASSPORT
- ❑ DRIVER'S LICENSE
- ❑ OTHER: _____
- ❑ CREDIBLE WITNESS
- ❑ KNOWN PERSONALLY

ID NUMBER:

ISSUED BY:

DATE ISSUED:　　　EXPIRATION DATE:

WITNESS FULL NAME:	PHONE NUMBER:
EMAIL ADDRESS:	WITNESS SIGNATURE:
ADDRESS:	

DOCUMENT TYPE:	DATE/TIME NOTARIZED:	DOCUMENT DATE:	FEE CHARGED:

COMMENTS:	RECORD NUMBER: **185**

NOTARY LOG

FULL NAME:	PHONE NUMBER:	THUMB PRINT
EMAIL ADDRESS:	SIGNER'S SIGNATURE	
ADDRESS:		

SERVICE PERFORMED:
- ❑ JURAT
- ❑ OATH
- ❑ ACKNOWLEDGEMENT
- ❑ OTHER: _____

IDENTIFICATION
- ❑ ID CARD
- ❑ PASSPORT
- ❑ DRIVER'S LICENSE
- ❑ OTHER: _____
- ❑ CREDIBLE WITNESS
- ❑ KNOWN PERSONALLY

ID NUMBER:

ISSUED BY:

DATE ISSUED:　　　EXPIRATION DATE:

WITNESS FULL NAME:	PHONE NUMBER:
EMAIL ADDRESS:	WITNESS SIGNATURE:
ADDRESS:	

DOCUMENT TYPE:	DATE/TIME NOTARIZED:	DOCUMENT DATE:	FEE CHARGED:

COMMENTS:	RECORD NUMBER: **186**

NOTARY LOG

FULL NAME:	PHONE NUMBER:	THUMB PRINT
EMAIL ADDRESS:	SIGNER'S SIGNATURE	
ADDRESS:		

SERVICE PERFORMED:
- ❏ JURAT
- ❏ OATH
- ❏ ACKNOWLEDGEMENT
- ❏ OTHER: _____

IDENTIFICATION
- ❏ ID CARD
- ❏ PASSPORT
- ❏ DRIVER'S LICENSE
- ❏ OTHER: _____
- ❏ CREDIBLE WITNESS
- ❏ KNOWN PERSONALLY

ID NUMBER:

ISSUED BY:

DATE ISSUED: | EXPIRATION DATE:

WITNESS FULL NAME:	PHONE NUMBER:
EMAIL ADDRESS:	WITNESS SIGNATURE:
ADDRESS:	

DOCUMENT TYPE:	DATE/TIME NOTARIZED:	DOCUMENT DATE:	FEE CHARGED:

COMMENTS:　　　　　　　　　　　　　　　　　RECORD NUMBER: **187**

NOTARY LOG

FULL NAME:	PHONE NUMBER:	THUMB PRINT
EMAIL ADDRESS:	SIGNER'S SIGNATURE	
ADDRESS:		

SERVICE PERFORMED:
- ❏ JURAT
- ❏ OATH
- ❏ ACKNOWLEDGEMENT
- ❏ OTHER: _____

IDENTIFICATION
- ❏ ID CARD
- ❏ PASSPORT
- ❏ DRIVER'S LICENSE
- ❏ OTHER: _____
- ❏ CREDIBLE WITNESS
- ❏ KNOWN PERSONALLY

ID NUMBER:

ISSUED BY:

DATE ISSUED: | EXPIRATION DATE:

WITNESS FULL NAME:	PHONE NUMBER:
EMAIL ADDRESS:	WITNESS SIGNATURE:
ADDRESS:	

DOCUMENT TYPE:	DATE/TIME NOTARIZED:	DOCUMENT DATE:	FEE CHARGED:

COMMENTS:　　　　　　　　　　　　　　　　　RECORD NUMBER: **188**

NOTARY LOG

FULL NAME:	PHONE NUMBER:	THUMB PRINT
EMAIL ADDRESS:	SIGNER'S SIGNATURE	
ADDRESS:		

SERVICE PERFORMED:
- ❏ JURAT
- ❏ OATH
- ❏ ACKNOWLEDGEMENT
- ❏ OTHER: _____

IDENTIFICATION
- ❏ ID CARD
- ❏ PASSPORT
- ❏ DRIVER'S LICENSE
- ❏ OTHER: _____
- ❏ CREDIBLE WITNESS
- ❏ KNOWN PERSONALLY

ID NUMBER:

ISSUED BY:

DATE ISSUED: | EXPIRATION DATE:

WITNESS FULL NAME:	PHONE NUMBER:
EMAIL ADDRESS:	WITNESS SIGNATURE:
ADDRESS:	

DOCUMENT TYPE:	DATE/TIME NOTARIZED:	DOCUMENT DATE:	FEE CHARGED:

COMMENTS:　　　　　　　　　　　　　　　　　　　　RECORD NUMBER: **189**

NOTARY LOG

FULL NAME:	PHONE NUMBER:	THUMB PRINT
EMAIL ADDRESS:	SIGNER'S SIGNATURE	
ADDRESS:		

SERVICE PERFORMED:
- ❏ JURAT
- ❏ OATH
- ❏ ACKNOWLEDGEMENT
- ❏ OTHER: _____

IDENTIFICATION
- ❏ ID CARD
- ❏ PASSPORT
- ❏ DRIVER'S LICENSE
- ❏ OTHER: _____
- ❏ CREDIBLE WITNESS
- ❏ KNOWN PERSONALLY

ID NUMBER:

ISSUED BY:

DATE ISSUED: | EXPIRATION DATE:

WITNESS FULL NAME:	PHONE NUMBER:
EMAIL ADDRESS:	WITNESS SIGNATURE:
ADDRESS:	

DOCUMENT TYPE:	DATE/TIME NOTARIZED:	DOCUMENT DATE:	FEE CHARGED:

COMMENTS:　　　　　　　　　　　　　　　　　　　　RECORD NUMBER: **190**

NOTARY LOG

FULL NAME:	PHONE NUMBER:	THUMB PRINT
EMAIL ADDRESS:	SIGNER'S SIGNATURE	
ADDRESS:		

SERVICE PERFORMED:
- ❑ JURAT
- ❑ OATH
- ❑ ACKNOWLEDGEMENT
- ❑ OTHER: _____

IDENTIFICATION
- ❑ ID CARD
- ❑ PASSPORT
- ❑ DRIVER'S LICENSE
- ❑ OTHER: _____
- ❑ CREDIBLE WITNESS
- ❑ KNOWN PERSONALLY

ID NUMBER:

ISSUED BY:

DATE ISSUED: | EXPIRATION DATE:

WITNESS FULL NAME:	PHONE NUMBER:
EMAIL ADDRESS:	WITNESS SIGNATURE:
ADDRESS:	

DOCUMENT TYPE:	DATE/TIME NOTARIZED:	DOCUMENT DATE:	FEE CHARGED:

COMMENTS:

RECORD NUMBER: **191**

NOTARY LOG

FULL NAME:	PHONE NUMBER:	THUMB PRINT
EMAIL ADDRESS:	SIGNER'S SIGNATURE	
ADDRESS:		

SERVICE PERFORMED:
- ❑ JURAT
- ❑ OATH
- ❑ ACKNOWLEDGEMENT
- ❑ OTHER: _____

IDENTIFICATION
- ❑ ID CARD
- ❑ PASSPORT
- ❑ DRIVER'S LICENSE
- ❑ OTHER: _____
- ❑ CREDIBLE WITNESS
- ❑ KNOWN PERSONALLY

ID NUMBER:

ISSUED BY:

DATE ISSUED: | EXPIRATION DATE:

WITNESS FULL NAME:	PHONE NUMBER:
EMAIL ADDRESS:	WITNESS SIGNATURE:
ADDRESS:	

DOCUMENT TYPE:	DATE/TIME NOTARIZED:	DOCUMENT DATE:	FEE CHARGED:

COMMENTS:

RECORD NUMBER: **192**

NOTARY LOG

FULL NAME:	PHONE NUMBER:	THUMB PRINT
EMAIL ADDRESS:	SIGNER'S SIGNATURE	
ADDRESS:		

SERVICE PERFORMED:
- ❑ JURAT
- ❑ OATH
- ❑ ACKNOWLEDGEMENT
- ❑ OTHER: _____

IDENTIFICATION
- ❑ ID CARD
- ❑ PASSPORT
- ❑ DRIVER'S LICENSE
- ❑ OTHER: _____
- ❑ CREDIBLE WITNESS
- ❑ KNOWN PERSONALLY

ID NUMBER:

ISSUED BY:

DATE ISSUED: EXPIRATION DATE:

WITNESS FULL NAME:	PHONE NUMBER:
EMAIL ADDRESS:	WITNESS SIGNATURE:
ADDRESS:	

DOCUMENT TYPE:	DATE/TIME NOTARIZED:	DOCUMENT DATE:	FEE CHARGED:
COMMENTS:			RECORD NUMBER: **193**

NOTARY LOG

FULL NAME:	PHONE NUMBER:	THUMB PRINT
EMAIL ADDRESS:	SIGNER'S SIGNATURE	
ADDRESS:		

SERVICE PERFORMED:
- ❑ JURAT
- ❑ OATH
- ❑ ACKNOWLEDGEMENT
- ❑ OTHER: _____

IDENTIFICATION
- ❑ ID CARD
- ❑ PASSPORT
- ❑ DRIVER'S LICENSE
- ❑ OTHER: _____
- ❑ CREDIBLE WITNESS
- ❑ KNOWN PERSONALLY

ID NUMBER:

ISSUED BY:

DATE ISSUED: EXPIRATION DATE:

WITNESS FULL NAME:	PHONE NUMBER:
EMAIL ADDRESS:	WITNESS SIGNATURE:
ADDRESS:	

DOCUMENT TYPE:	DATE/TIME NOTARIZED:	DOCUMENT DATE:	FEE CHARGED:
COMMENTS:			RECORD NUMBER: **194**

NOTARY LOG

FULL NAME:	PHONE NUMBER:	THUMB PRINT
EMAIL ADDRESS:	SIGNER'S SIGNATURE	
ADDRESS:		

SERVICE PERFORMED:
- ❑ JURAT
- ❑ OATH
- ❑ ACKNOWLEDGEMENT
- ❑ OTHER: _____

IDENTIFICATION
- ❑ ID CARD
- ❑ PASSPORT
- ❑ DRIVER'S LICENSE
- ❑ OTHER: _____
- ❑ CREDIBLE WITNESS
- ❑ KNOWN PERSONALLY

ID NUMBER:

ISSUED BY:

DATE ISSUED: EXPIRATION DATE:

WITNESS FULL NAME:	PHONE NUMBER:
EMAIL ADDRESS:	WITNESS SIGNATURE:
ADDRESS:	

DOCUMENT TYPE:	DATE/TIME NOTARIZED:	DOCUMENT DATE:	FEE CHARGED:

COMMENTS:		RECORD NUMBER: 195

NOTARY LOG

FULL NAME:	PHONE NUMBER:	THUMB PRINT
EMAIL ADDRESS:	SIGNER'S SIGNATURE	
ADDRESS:		

SERVICE PERFORMED:
- ❑ JURAT
- ❑ OATH
- ❑ ACKNOWLEDGEMENT
- ❑ OTHER: _____

IDENTIFICATION
- ❑ ID CARD
- ❑ PASSPORT
- ❑ DRIVER'S LICENSE
- ❑ OTHER: _____
- ❑ CREDIBLE WITNESS
- ❑ KNOWN PERSONALLY

ID NUMBER:

ISSUED BY:

DATE ISSUED: EXPIRATION DATE:

WITNESS FULL NAME:	PHONE NUMBER:
EMAIL ADDRESS:	WITNESS SIGNATURE:
ADDRESS:	

DOCUMENT TYPE:	DATE/TIME NOTARIZED:	DOCUMENT DATE:	FEE CHARGED:

COMMENTS:		RECORD NUMBER: 196

NOTARY LOG

FULL NAME:	PHONE NUMBER:	THUMB PRINT
EMAIL ADDRESS:	SIGNER'S SIGNATURE	
ADDRESS:		

SERVICE PERFORMED:
- ❑ JURAT
- ❑ OATH
- ❑ ACKNOWLEDGEMENT
- ❑ OTHER: _____

IDENTIFICATION
- ❑ ID CARD
- ❑ PASSPORT
- ❑ DRIVER'S LICENSE
- ❑ OTHER: _____
- ❑ CREDIBLE WITNESS
- ❑ KNOWN PERSONALLY

ID NUMBER:

ISSUED BY:

DATE ISSUED: EXPIRATION DATE:

WITNESS FULL NAME:	PHONE NUMBER:
EMAIL ADDRESS:	WITNESS SIGNATURE:
ADDRESS:	

DOCUMENT TYPE:	DATE/TIME NOTARIZED:	DOCUMENT DATE:	FEE CHARGED:

COMMENTS:

RECORD NUMBER: **197**

NOTARY LOG

FULL NAME:	PHONE NUMBER:	THUMB PRINT
EMAIL ADDRESS:	SIGNER'S SIGNATURE	
ADDRESS:		

SERVICE PERFORMED:
- ❑ JURAT
- ❑ OATH
- ❑ ACKNOWLEDGEMENT
- ❑ OTHER: _____

IDENTIFICATION
- ❑ ID CARD
- ❑ PASSPORT
- ❑ DRIVER'S LICENSE
- ❑ OTHER: _____
- ❑ CREDIBLE WITNESS
- ❑ KNOWN PERSONALLY

ID NUMBER:

ISSUED BY:

DATE ISSUED: EXPIRATION DATE:

WITNESS FULL NAME:	PHONE NUMBER:
EMAIL ADDRESS:	WITNESS SIGNATURE:
ADDRESS:	

DOCUMENT TYPE:	DATE/TIME NOTARIZED:	DOCUMENT DATE:	FEE CHARGED:

COMMENTS:

RECORD NUMBER: **198**

NOTARY LOG

FULL NAME:	PHONE NUMBER:	THUMB PRINT
EMAIL ADDRESS:	SIGNER'S SIGNATURE	
ADDRESS:		

SERVICE PERFORMED:
- ❏ JURAT
- ❏ OATH
- ❏ ACKNOWLEDGEMENT
- ❏ OTHER: _____

IDENTIFICATION
- ❏ ID CARD
- ❏ PASSPORT
- ❏ DRIVER'S LICENSE
- ❏ OTHER: _____
- ❏ CREDIBLE WITNESS
- ❏ KNOWN PERSONALLY

ID NUMBER:

ISSUED BY:

DATE ISSUED:	EXPIRATION DATE:

WITNESS FULL NAME:	PHONE NUMBER:
EMAIL ADDRESS:	WITNESS SIGNATURE:
ADDRESS:	

DOCUMENT TYPE:	DATE/TIME NOTARIZED:	DOCUMENT DATE:	FEE CHARGED:

COMMENTS:		RECORD NUMBER: **199**

NOTARY LOG

FULL NAME:	PHONE NUMBER:	THUMB PRINT
EMAIL ADDRESS:	SIGNER'S SIGNATURE	
ADDRESS:		

SERVICE PERFORMED:
- ❏ JURAT
- ❏ OATH
- ❏ ACKNOWLEDGEMENT
- ❏ OTHER: _____

IDENTIFICATION
- ❏ ID CARD
- ❏ PASSPORT
- ❏ DRIVER'S LICENSE
- ❏ OTHER: _____
- ❏ CREDIBLE WITNESS
- ❏ KNOWN PERSONALLY

ID NUMBER:

ISSUED BY:

DATE ISSUED:	EXPIRATION DATE:

WITNESS FULL NAME:	PHONE NUMBER:
EMAIL ADDRESS:	WITNESS SIGNATURE:
ADDRESS:	

DOCUMENT TYPE:	DATE/TIME NOTARIZED:	DOCUMENT DATE:	FEE CHARGED:

COMMENTS:		RECORD NUMBER: **200**

NOTARY LOG

FULL NAME:

PHONE NUMBER:

THUMB PRINT

EMAIL ADDRESS:

SIGNER'S SIGNATURE

ADDRESS:

SERVICE PERFORMED:

- ❑ JURAT
- ❑ OATH
- ❑ ACKNOWLEDGEMENT
- ❑ OTHER: _____

IDENTIFICATION

- ❑ ID CARD
- ❑ PASSPORT
- ❑ DRIVER'S LICENSE
- ❑ OTHER: _____
- ❑ CREDIBLE WITNESS
- ❑ KNOWN PERSONALLY

ID NUMBER:

ISSUED BY:

DATE ISSUED:

EXPIRATION DATE:

WITNESS FULL NAME:

PHONE NUMBER:

EMAIL ADDRESS:

WITNESS SIGNATURE:

ADDRESS:

DOCUMENT TYPE:	DATE/TIME NOTARIZED:	DOCUMENT DATE:	FEE CHARGED:

COMMENTS:

RECORD NUMBER: 201

NOTARY LOG

FULL NAME:

PHONE NUMBER:

THUMB PRINT

EMAIL ADDRESS:

SIGNER'S SIGNATURE

ADDRESS:

SERVICE PERFORMED:

- ❑ JURAT
- ❑ OATH
- ❑ ACKNOWLEDGEMENT
- ❑ OTHER: _____

IDENTIFICATION

- ❑ ID CARD
- ❑ PASSPORT
- ❑ DRIVER'S LICENSE
- ❑ OTHER: _____
- ❑ CREDIBLE WITNESS
- ❑ KNOWN PERSONALLY

ID NUMBER:

ISSUED BY:

DATE ISSUED:

EXPIRATION DATE:

WITNESS FULL NAME:

PHONE NUMBER:

EMAIL ADDRESS:

WITNESS SIGNATURE:

ADDRESS:

DOCUMENT TYPE:	DATE/TIME NOTARIZED:	DOCUMENT DATE:	FEE CHARGED:

COMMENTS:

RECORD NUMBER: 202

NOTARY LOG

FULL NAME:

PHONE NUMBER:

THUMB PRINT

EMAIL ADDRESS:

SIGNER'S SIGNATURE

ADDRESS:

SERVICE PERFORMED:
- ❏ JURAT
- ❏ OATH
- ❏ ACKNOWLEDGEMENT
- ❏ OTHER: _____

IDENTIFICATION
- ❏ ID CARD
- ❏ PASSPORT
- ❏ DRIVER'S LICENSE
- ❏ OTHER: _____
- ❏ CREDIBLE WITNESS
- ❏ KNOWN PERSONALLY

ID NUMBER:

ISSUED BY:

DATE ISSUED:

EXPIRATION DATE:

WITNESS FULL NAME:

PHONE NUMBER:

EMAIL ADDRESS:

WITNESS SIGNATURE:

ADDRESS:

DOCUMENT TYPE:

DATE/TIME NOTARIZED:

DOCUMENT DATE:

FEE CHARGED:

COMMENTS:

RECORD NUMBER: 203

NOTARY LOG

FULL NAME:

PHONE NUMBER:

THUMB PRINT

EMAIL ADDRESS:

SIGNER'S SIGNATURE

ADDRESS:

SERVICE PERFORMED:
- ❏ JURAT
- ❏ OATH
- ❏ ACKNOWLEDGEMENT
- ❏ OTHER: _____

IDENTIFICATION
- ❏ ID CARD
- ❏ PASSPORT
- ❏ DRIVER'S LICENSE
- ❏ OTHER: _____
- ❏ CREDIBLE WITNESS
- ❏ KNOWN PERSONALLY

ID NUMBER:

ISSUED BY:

DATE ISSUED:

EXPIRATION DATE:

WITNESS FULL NAME:

PHONE NUMBER:

EMAIL ADDRESS:

WITNESS SIGNATURE:

ADDRESS:

DOCUMENT TYPE:

DATE/TIME NOTARIZED:

DOCUMENT DATE:

FEE CHARGED:

COMMENTS:

RECORD NUMBER: 204

NOTARY LOG

FULL NAME:

PHONE NUMBER:

THUMB PRINT

EMAIL ADDRESS:

SIGNER'S SIGNATURE

ADDRESS:

SERVICE PERFORMED:
- ☐ JURAT
- ☐ OATH
- ☐ ACKNOWLEDGEMENT
- ☐ OTHER: _____

IDENTIFICATION
- ☐ ID CARD
- ☐ PASSPORT
- ☐ DRIVER'S LICENSE
- ☐ OTHER: _____
- ☐ CREDIBLE WITNESS
- ☐ KNOWN PERSONALLY

ID NUMBER:

ISSUED BY:

DATE ISSUED:

EXPIRATION DATE:

WITNESS FULL NAME:

PHONE NUMBER:

EMAIL ADDRESS:

WITNESS SIGNATURE:

ADDRESS:

DOCUMENT TYPE:	DATE/TIME NOTARIZED:	DOCUMENT DATE:	FEE CHARGED:

COMMENTS:

RECORD NUMBER: 205

NOTARY LOG

FULL NAME:

PHONE NUMBER:

THUMB PRINT

EMAIL ADDRESS:

SIGNER'S SIGNATURE

ADDRESS:

SERVICE PERFORMED:
- ☐ JURAT
- ☐ OATH
- ☐ ACKNOWLEDGEMENT
- ☐ OTHER: _____

IDENTIFICATION
- ☐ ID CARD
- ☐ PASSPORT
- ☐ DRIVER'S LICENSE
- ☐ OTHER: _____
- ☐ CREDIBLE WITNESS
- ☐ KNOWN PERSONALLY

ID NUMBER:

ISSUED BY:

DATE ISSUED:

EXPIRATION DATE:

WITNESS FULL NAME:

PHONE NUMBER:

EMAIL ADDRESS:

WITNESS SIGNATURE:

ADDRESS:

DOCUMENT TYPE:	DATE/TIME NOTARIZED:	DOCUMENT DATE:	FEE CHARGED:

COMMENTS:

RECORD NUMBER: 206

NOTARY LOG

FULL NAME:	PHONE NUMBER:	THUMB PRINT
EMAIL ADDRESS:	SIGNER'S SIGNATURE	
ADDRESS:		

SERVICE PERFORMED:
- ❑ JURAT
- ❑ OATH
- ❑ ACKNOWLEDGEMENT
- ❑ OTHER: _____

IDENTIFICATION
- ❑ ID CARD
- ❑ PASSPORT
- ❑ DRIVER'S LICENSE
- ❑ OTHER: _____
- ❑ CREDIBLE WITNESS
- ❑ KNOWN PERSONALLY

ID NUMBER:

ISSUED BY:

DATE ISSUED: EXPIRATION DATE:

WITNESS FULL NAME:	PHONE NUMBER:
EMAIL ADDRESS:	WITNESS SIGNATURE:
ADDRESS:	

DOCUMENT TYPE:	DATE/TIME NOTARIZED:	DOCUMENT DATE:	FEE CHARGED:

COMMENTS:

RECORD NUMBER: **207**

NOTARY LOG

FULL NAME:	PHONE NUMBER:	THUMB PRINT
EMAIL ADDRESS:	SIGNER'S SIGNATURE	
ADDRESS:		

SERVICE PERFORMED:
- ❑ JURAT
- ❑ OATH
- ❑ ACKNOWLEDGEMENT
- ❑ OTHER: _____

IDENTIFICATION
- ❑ ID CARD
- ❑ PASSPORT
- ❑ DRIVER'S LICENSE
- ❑ OTHER: _____
- ❑ CREDIBLE WITNESS
- ❑ KNOWN PERSONALLY

ID NUMBER:

ISSUED BY:

DATE ISSUED: EXPIRATION DATE:

WITNESS FULL NAME:	PHONE NUMBER:
EMAIL ADDRESS:	WITNESS SIGNATURE:
ADDRESS:	

DOCUMENT TYPE:	DATE/TIME NOTARIZED:	DOCUMENT DATE:	FEE CHARGED:

COMMENTS:

RECORD NUMBER: **208**

NOTARY LOG

FULL NAME:

PHONE NUMBER:

THUMB PRINT

EMAIL ADDRESS:

SIGNER'S SIGNATURE

ADDRESS:

SERVICE PERFORMED:
- ❑ JURAT
- ❑ OATH
- ❑ ACKNOWLEDGEMENT
- ❑ OTHER: _____

IDENTIFICATION
- ❑ ID CARD
- ❑ PASSPORT
- ❑ DRIVER'S LICENSE
- ❑ OTHER: _____
- ❑ CREDIBLE WITNESS
- ❑ KNOWN PERSONALLY

ID NUMBER:

ISSUED BY:

DATE ISSUED:

EXPIRATION DATE:

WITNESS FULL NAME:

PHONE NUMBER:

EMAIL ADDRESS:

WITNESS SIGNATURE:

ADDRESS:

DOCUMENT TYPE:

DATE/TIME NOTARIZED:

DOCUMENT DATE:

FEE CHARGED:

COMMENTS:

RECORD NUMBER: 209

NOTARY LOG

FULL NAME:

PHONE NUMBER:

THUMB PRINT

EMAIL ADDRESS:

SIGNER'S SIGNATURE

ADDRESS:

SERVICE PERFORMED:
- ❑ JURAT
- ❑ OATH
- ❑ ACKNOWLEDGEMENT
- ❑ OTHER: _____

IDENTIFICATION
- ❑ ID CARD
- ❑ PASSPORT
- ❑ DRIVER'S LICENSE
- ❑ OTHER: _____
- ❑ CREDIBLE WITNESS
- ❑ KNOWN PERSONALLY

ID NUMBER:

ISSUED BY:

DATE ISSUED:

EXPIRATION DATE:

WITNESS FULL NAME:

PHONE NUMBER:

EMAIL ADDRESS:

WITNESS SIGNATURE:

ADDRESS:

DOCUMENT TYPE:

DATE/TIME NOTARIZED:

DOCUMENT DATE:

FEE CHARGED:

COMMENTS:

RECORD NUMBER: 210

NOTARY LOG

FULL NAME:	PHONE NUMBER:	THUMB PRINT

EMAIL ADDRESS:

ADDRESS:

SIGNER'S SIGNATURE

SERVICE PERFORMED:
- ❏ JURAT
- ❏ OATH
- ❏ ACKNOWLEDGEMENT
- ❏ OTHER: _____

IDENTIFICATION
- ❏ ID CARD
- ❏ PASSPORT
- ❏ DRIVER'S LICENSE
- ❏ OTHER: _____
- ❏ CREDIBLE WITNESS
- ❏ KNOWN PERSONALLY

ID NUMBER:

ISSUED BY:

DATE ISSUED: | **EXPIRATION DATE:**

WITNESS FULL NAME: | **PHONE NUMBER:**

EMAIL ADDRESS:

ADDRESS:

WITNESS SIGNATURE:

DOCUMENT TYPE:	DATE/TIME NOTARIZED:	DOCUMENT DATE:	FEE CHARGED:

COMMENTS:

RECORD NUMBER: 211

NOTARY LOG

FULL NAME:	PHONE NUMBER:	THUMB PRINT

EMAIL ADDRESS:

ADDRESS:

SIGNER'S SIGNATURE

SERVICE PERFORMED:
- ❏ JURAT
- ❏ OATH
- ❏ ACKNOWLEDGEMENT
- ❏ OTHER: _____

IDENTIFICATION
- ❏ ID CARD
- ❏ PASSPORT
- ❏ DRIVER'S LICENSE
- ❏ OTHER: _____
- ❏ CREDIBLE WITNESS
- ❏ KNOWN PERSONALLY

ID NUMBER:

ISSUED BY:

DATE ISSUED: | **EXPIRATION DATE:**

WITNESS FULL NAME: | **PHONE NUMBER:**

EMAIL ADDRESS:

ADDRESS:

WITNESS SIGNATURE:

DOCUMENT TYPE:	DATE/TIME NOTARIZED:	DOCUMENT DATE:	FEE CHARGED:

COMMENTS:

RECORD NUMBER: 212

NOTARY LOG

FULL NAME:	PHONE NUMBER:	THUMB PRINT
EMAIL ADDRESS:	SIGNER'S SIGNATURE	
ADDRESS:		

SERVICE PERFORMED:
- ❑ JURAT
- ❑ OATH
- ❑ ACKNOWLEDGEMENT
- ❑ OTHER: _____

IDENTIFICATION
- ❑ ID CARD
- ❑ PASSPORT
- ❑ DRIVER'S LICENSE
- ❑ OTHER: _____
- ❑ CREDIBLE WITNESS
- ❑ KNOWN PERSONALLY

ID NUMBER:

ISSUED BY:

DATE ISSUED: EXPIRATION DATE:

WITNESS FULL NAME:	PHONE NUMBER:
EMAIL ADDRESS:	WITNESS SIGNATURE:
ADDRESS:	

DOCUMENT TYPE:	DATE/TIME NOTARIZED:	DOCUMENT DATE:	FEE CHARGED:

COMMENTS:

RECORD NUMBER: **213**

NOTARY LOG

FULL NAME:	PHONE NUMBER:	THUMB PRINT
EMAIL ADDRESS:	SIGNER'S SIGNATURE	
ADDRESS:		

SERVICE PERFORMED:
- ❑ JURAT
- ❑ OATH
- ❑ ACKNOWLEDGEMENT
- ❑ OTHER: _____

IDENTIFICATION
- ❑ ID CARD
- ❑ PASSPORT
- ❑ DRIVER'S LICENSE
- ❑ OTHER: _____
- ❑ CREDIBLE WITNESS
- ❑ KNOWN PERSONALLY

ID NUMBER:

ISSUED BY:

DATE ISSUED: EXPIRATION DATE:

WITNESS FULL NAME:	PHONE NUMBER:
EMAIL ADDRESS:	WITNESS SIGNATURE:
ADDRESS:	

DOCUMENT TYPE:	DATE/TIME NOTARIZED:	DOCUMENT DATE:	FEE CHARGED:

COMMENTS:

RECORD NUMBER: **214**

NOTARY LOG

FULL NAME:	PHONE NUMBER:	THUMB PRINT
EMAIL ADDRESS:	SIGNER'S SIGNATURE	
ADDRESS:		

SERVICE PERFORMED:
- ❑ JURAT
- ❑ OATH
- ❑ ACKNOWLEDGEMENT
- ❑ OTHER: _____

IDENTIFICATION
- ❑ ID CARD
- ❑ PASSPORT
- ❑ DRIVER'S LICENSE
- ❑ OTHER: _____
- ❑ CREDIBLE WITNESS
- ❑ KNOWN PERSONALLY

ID NUMBER:

ISSUED BY:

DATE ISSUED:

EXPIRATION DATE:

WITNESS FULL NAME:	PHONE NUMBER:
EMAIL ADDRESS:	WITNESS SIGNATURE:
ADDRESS:	

DOCUMENT TYPE:	DATE/TIME NOTARIZED:	DOCUMENT DATE:	FEE CHARGED:
COMMENTS:			RECORD NUMBER: **215**

NOTARY LOG

FULL NAME:	PHONE NUMBER:	THUMB PRINT
EMAIL ADDRESS:	SIGNER'S SIGNATURE	
ADDRESS:		

SERVICE PERFORMED:
- ❑ JURAT
- ❑ OATH
- ❑ ACKNOWLEDGEMENT
- ❑ OTHER: _____

IDENTIFICATION
- ❑ ID CARD
- ❑ PASSPORT
- ❑ DRIVER'S LICENSE
- ❑ OTHER: _____
- ❑ CREDIBLE WITNESS
- ❑ KNOWN PERSONALLY

ID NUMBER:

ISSUED BY:

DATE ISSUED:

EXPIRATION DATE:

WITNESS FULL NAME:	PHONE NUMBER:
EMAIL ADDRESS:	WITNESS SIGNATURE:
ADDRESS:	

DOCUMENT TYPE:	DATE/TIME NOTARIZED:	DOCUMENT DATE:	FEE CHARGED:
COMMENTS:			RECORD NUMBER: **216**

NOTARY LOG

FULL NAME:	PHONE NUMBER:	THUMB PRINT
EMAIL ADDRESS:	SIGNER'S SIGNATURE	
ADDRESS:		

SERVICE PERFORMED:
- ❏ JURAT
- ❏ OATH
- ❏ ACKNOWLEDGEMENT
- ❏ OTHER: _____

IDENTIFICATION
- ❏ ID CARD
- ❏ PASSPORT
- ❏ DRIVER'S LICENSE
- ❏ OTHER: _____
- ❏ CREDIBLE WITNESS
- ❏ KNOWN PERSONALLY

ID NUMBER:

ISSUED BY:

DATE ISSUED: EXPIRATION DATE:

WITNESS FULL NAME:	PHONE NUMBER:
EMAIL ADDRESS:	WITNESS SIGNATURE:
ADDRESS:	

DOCUMENT TYPE:	DATE/TIME NOTARIZED:	DOCUMENT DATE:	FEE CHARGED:

COMMENTS: RECORD NUMBER: 217

NOTARY LOG

FULL NAME:	PHONE NUMBER:	THUMB PRINT
EMAIL ADDRESS:	SIGNER'S SIGNATURE	
ADDRESS:		

SERVICE PERFORMED:
- ❏ JURAT
- ❏ OATH
- ❏ ACKNOWLEDGEMENT
- ❏ OTHER: _____

IDENTIFICATION
- ❏ ID CARD
- ❏ PASSPORT
- ❏ DRIVER'S LICENSE
- ❏ OTHER: _____
- ❏ CREDIBLE WITNESS
- ❏ KNOWN PERSONALLY

ID NUMBER:

ISSUED BY:

DATE ISSUED: EXPIRATION DATE:

WITNESS FULL NAME:	PHONE NUMBER:
EMAIL ADDRESS:	WITNESS SIGNATURE:
ADDRESS:	

DOCUMENT TYPE:	DATE/TIME NOTARIZED:	DOCUMENT DATE:	FEE CHARGED:

COMMENTS: RECORD NUMBER: 218

Made in United States
Orlando, FL
20 October 2024

52937947R00061